Answering the Call

Candidacy Guidebook

HIGHER EDUCATION & MINISTRY
General Board of Higher Education and Ministry
THE UNITED METHODIST CHURCH

Answering the Call

Candidacy Guidebook

The General Board of Higher Education and Ministry leads and serves The United Methodist Church in the recruitment, preparation, nurture, education, and support of Christian leaders—lay and clergy—for the work of making disciples of Jesus Christ in the Transformation of the World.

Division of Ordained Ministry
General Board of Higher Education and Ministry
The United Methodist Church
PO Box 340007
Nashville, TN 37203-0007

Editorial Board: Meg Lassiat • Anna Masi • Helen Neinast

ISBN 978-0-938162-67-4

Produced by the Office of Communications.

Table of Contents

Foreword

Dear Friend in Christ,

We at the General Board of Higher Education and Ministry are pleased that you are on a spiritual journey of discerning your call to ministry. This Candidacy Guidebook is just that, a resource that we believe will help you ask the questions you must faithfully and truthfully answer for yourself and your family as you respond to God's call. I hope you will use the Candidacy Guidebook as a map for the territory.

Christ's call is very strong, and surely you are hearing it. The question is not "Is God calling you to ministry?" The question is, "Do you have the gifts, grace, and fruits for 'ordained' ministry?" A Big Question. A Big Decision. Whatever your answer is, know this: God will use you.

As you align your life with God's purposes, I am sure that what God has begun in you, He will bring to completion. In the words of the great poet and Pulitzer Prize winner, Mary Oliver, you are in our prayers as you find your way forward in your *precious* life.

The Rev. Dr. Kim Cape
General Secretary
General Board of Higher Education and Ministry

Acknowledgments

Many people were involved in making this book what it is. We extend our gratitude to the General Board of Pension and Health Benefits for their assistance with the Health and Wholeness and Financial Literacy chapters and the resources they provided.

In addition, we are indebted to our reading team, who pruned back our drafts and helped us see with fresh eyes. Amy Aspey, Marcus Freeman, Kim Ingram, John Edd Harper, and Thomas Mattick: thank you for your time, your wisdom, and your dedication.

PART I
Discerning the Call

One of the oldest symbols in the Christian tradition is that of the mother pelican feeding her young. She is lesser known in Christianity today, but if you look closely, you will find her. She looks down daily on passing pedestrians in Paris, nestled between the gargoyles atop Notre Dame. She is perched on a table in a small chapel inside St. Michael and St. Gudula Cathedral in Brussels. In a sanctuary mural at The Cathedral of the Madeleine in Salt Lake City, she stands beneath the cross. Her pose is always the same: she stands upright with her wings outstretched and her beak pointed down into her chest, her children flocking around her, looking up at her expectantly.

The story behind the mother pelican predates Christianity. In ancient times, legend held that mother pelicans, when they could not feed their young, would lean down, pierce their own chests with their beaks, and sustain their babies with their own blood. Unsurprisingly, for Christians this imagery recalled

Christ's death and resurrection, and the way Christ continues to sustain God's people through Holy Communion.[1]

In many ways, this is also a wonderful image of ministry. Ministry involves the many ways we share with others God's grace. All believers are called to share Christ's life-giving love with the world, often giving of ourselves to sustain those around us. It happens in churches and coffee shops, choir rooms and living rooms, in schools, in hospitals, on sidewalks.

You come to this time in your life to focus on your place in the ministry of all believers. Slowing down, making time for reflection and prayer, practicing how to listen with both your heart and your head: these are some of the ways you will be invited to understand better who you are—and who God is calling you to be.

Calls are both subtle and obvious. Hearing and understanding a call can be a clear and gentle process or an unsettling one. John Schuster (whose calls included teaching in Chicago's inner city, working for the Environmental Protection Agency, and consulting with businesses on leadership development) knew something about calling. "Answering a call will bring mentors into your life. It will also bring tormentors," he said.[2]

Whether you encounter clarity or confusion, mentors or tormentors, one thing is certain: always—*always*—God goes with you and keeps you close, perhaps especially in those places on your journey when you are least able to feel God's presence.

So now you are welcomed into a community of seekers—other United Methodists who are exploring their calls. Within this community, you will have a mentor who is also on this journey to seek and to know, and who will, along with your candidacy group, encourage, challenge, and support you.

As you begin the candidacy and mentoring process, as part of either a small group or in individual meetings, you will be offered time to:

- Discern and gain more clarity about your vocation, your ministry, and your call;
- Explore and experience a variety of spiritual disciplines to hone your practice of discernment;
- Develop a better understanding of The United Methodist Church (UMC), its heritage and practices, as well as how your call might be suited to this community;
- Reflect theologically on whether God is calling you to serve as a deacon, elder, local pastor, or layperson, and how you can best respond to God's call.

At the end of each section are reflection questions and resources for further reading and consideration. You will find additional resources and detailed information about the steps for candidacy, licensing, and ordination in the appendices at the back of the book.

May this resource energize and guide you in the months ahead as you work toward understanding and responding to God's call. Enter this study with prayer and know that others in the church are praying for you, too. Remember, even as you seek God, God is seeking you.

Chapter One
Mentoring and Candidacy Groups

Larger-than-life historic persons like . . . [Native American visionary and healer] Black Elk provide dramatic examples of persons . . . who become mediators of the sacred to others. . . . It might be that a very ordinary person in the circle of our everyday life . . . serves as a prophetic truthteller . . . [and] shakes us up and challenges us to think about our life priorities in a new way. It could also be someone who appears as an angel of mercy in a time of pain or need, who speaks just the consoling words we need to hear . . . who gives us just the kind of advice or perspective we need in a time of personal confusion or darkness.

—John Neafsey[3]

Mentoring

The heart of your time in candidacy lies in spiritual discernment through personal reflection and in the relationships you establish with those you meet along the way. These relationships will challenge and console you and give you new perspectives on life. God will use many instruments to help you through your discernment; one of the most important will be your mentor and your candidacy group, who will accompany you in the coming weeks and months.

Candidacy mentors are trained to give counsel and guidance and to create a hospitable place for reflection and growth. With your mentor and your candidacy group, you will have the chance to discuss many issues and questions in a supportive setting. At its best, this experience can provide the freedom, confidentiality, flexibility, and stability that will lead to your deeper understanding of a call to licensed or ordained ministry. This time of companionship and guidance can open you to the Holy Spirit's leading in your decision-making.

Your mentor works with you and your candidacy group as a co-discerner and consultant to encourage and support you. She or he is also a representative of the Church who will help you explore The United Methodist Church's understanding of ministry, its teaching, and its polity and governance. These are important; they are the framework under which you will serve and lead if you represent and serve Christ through the UMC.

While mentors are a gift to the candidate, being in the role of candidate is also a gift. This time will give you perspective and the support you will need to understand who you are and how you might live as an ordained, licensed, or lay minister. It will also give you insight into the work you need to do in order to embrace your gifts, let go of any stumbling blocks, and gather the best in yourself for a life of ministry.

A Mutual Commitment

When you begin a relationship with your mentor and candidacy group, you make a commitment that involves trust, honesty, and integrity. Your commitment is to explore all aspects of your spirituality and calling, to ask for what you need, and to pray for each other. In turn, your mentor and group make the same commitment to you.

You, your mentor, and the others in your group will spend a lot of time together on this part of your journey. There will be many opportunities for growth, greater understanding, and surprising insights. Cherish these sacred relationships. Ask God to be present so that you can be open to hearing your sacred call.

Confidentiality with Other Candidates

The ethical principle of confidentiality here means that mutual trust among you, your mentor, and the members of your candidacy group is paramount. Confidentiality means having respect for each other and safeguarding what others say or disclose to group members. It includes listening carefully and empathetically. Confidentiality inspires a willingness to confide and a commitment to be worthy of shared confidences. Holding these confidences with great care honors God's intention for us to be in relationships that lend support and encouragement.

Confidentiality with Mentors

Mentors also have responsibilities both to you as a candidate and to the wider Church. Mentors are guides, consultants, advisors, and supporters; they serve the Church by guiding candidates through the candidacy process and helping candidates discern how they can best serve. As you prepare to interview with the district Committee on Ordained Ministry (dCOM), your mentor will share with committee members a written report. Introductory and informational, the report introduces you to the committee, outlines issues that may need exploring, and highlights your understanding of the gifts and grace you bring to ministry.

Your mentor prepares this report and shares it with you *before* sending it, and you and your mentor will consent to the content of the report. It will not contain any confidential information without your permission. In fact, no conversation or personal information is shared in the report unless *you* give written permission. Mutual respect and confidentiality are the baseline for the report, and in Chapter 9 of this resource you will find some suggestions to guide how this report is prepared.

Presence

You and the members of your candidacy group promise to be present at each meeting, to prepare thoughtfully, thoroughly, and prayerfully. You will all covenant to be fully present at each meeting, setting aside outside distractions as much as possible. Mentors and candidates alike will strive to fully engage through holy speaking and holy listening.

Participate with Hospitality

Group members will be welcoming and respectful to others' thoughts, feelings, and beliefs. Honesty, passion, compassion, and candor should characterize your mentoring conversations. Members approach each session with the belief that all have things to learn, and all have things to share. You, your mentor, and your group will practice mutuality in providing the physical, emotional, spiritual, and intellectual nourishment of your life together.

Prayer and Support

Candidates and mentors will pledge to hold one another in prayer, when together and while apart. This means taking time to understand what is happening in each other's lives. It also means being attentive to when prayer is needed, for individual needs and for the group's process and relationships.

Pledge to be Open

"God's Spirit blows wherever it wishes. You hear its sound, but you don't know where it comes from or where it is going. It's the same with everyone who is born of the Spirit" (John 3:8).[4] Take comfort; the Spirit infuses you and your candidacy group in all your conversations. Be ready for challenges—these, too, are marks of the Holy Spirit at work. Speak—even when you are not altogether sure about what you need to say. Listen carefully—the Spirit truly does blow where it wills. Be open and available to hear God and God's guidance for you.

Take Responsibility for Your Journey

This process is a part of your response to God's call in your life. Your mentors are also living into their own calls, which also make demands on their time and priorities. As you begin this journey, be sure you have a clear understanding of your responsibilities and important deadlines along the way. Be flexible and adaptable as you receive requirements, ask questions if you need clarity, and be clear with your mentor about commitments each of you will follow up on.

Covenants

You and your mentor or candidacy group will need to agree on the kind of relationship that will be most helpful as you embark on this journey together. Creating a covenant together can help define important boundaries and expectations for the work you will do together. Here are some suggestions to help create your covenant:

- Discuss and clarify agreed pledges to one another regarding confidentiality.
- Share mutual expectations and hopes, as well as limitations each may have. Expectations can also include a commitment to meeting times and deadlines.
- Identify which sections of this resource you anticipate will benefit each of you the most during the discernment and candidacy process. Commit to work through each session together in a spirit of openness, honesty, and support.
- In the spirit of openness and support, pledge to be open to the possibility of modifying your covenant, if necessary, as discernment progresses.

The Retreat

Your annual conference may offer a retreat or other gathering as part of the candidacy process. A retreat offers time away and encourages many creative possibilities for prayer, reflection, and fellowship. This is a time set apart for you to engage in dialogue, search for truth, embrace the sacred, learn about the logistics of the candidacy process, and explore your call.

For some United Methodist conferences, this retreat may be a conference-wide event. Many annual conferences now begin the candidacy process by inviting you, the other candidates, and mentors to a 24- or 48-hour retreat where you and other candidates meet with your group for the first time, begin the discernment process, and become oriented to the conference's expectations of you as a candidate.

At this retreat you will also learn what next steps are ahead for you. These range from psychological assessments to background checks to interviews with the district Committee to scheduling meetings with your mentor. While *The Book of Discipline of The United Methodist Church*[5] lists requirements common to all candidates, some conferences have additional requirements. You will hear of these at the candidacy retreat as well.

This retreat format is part of the process for many conferences. However, other conferences may choose to structure the retreat or gathering differently. No matter the structure, this is an important time away for discerning your call. It is a break from the constant barrage of information and media bombarding us all.

Embrace this retreat. Refresh your spirit. Let go of what you think you know. Lay out your call before God. Trust where your time apart will take you. Invite the Spirit to accompany you. Use your imagination as you listen to others' stories of their callings. Speak your own thoughts out loud. Pray for guidance. Listen for God. Approach this retreat as sacred time. Allow yourself to be blessed and strengthened. You have a lot ahead of you; time away in retreat is a gift for the journey.

Chapter Two
What United Methodists Believe: Our Theological Task, General Rules, Connectionalism, Mission, and the Social Principles

Christian intellectual life is the inheritance of every Christian and the calling on every believer to reflect deeply about their faith from the sites in this world that matter—where lives are at stake, and hope hangs in the balance.
> —Willie James Jennings[6]

An ounce of love is worth a pound of knowledge.
> —John Wesley[7]

In some ways, the quote above is a good summary of John Wesley's theology. He was a thoughtful theologian, but the Wesleyan movement was not about reformulating doctrine. The theological heritage we have from Wesley includes a strong integration of *practical* divinity, which is the call for believers to not only believe in Christianity, but to demonstrate our faith in action by how we live our lives. Wesley's urgent emphasis on living the Christian life—which he understood as faith and love put into practice—was the heart of his theology.

To understand Wesley, it is critical to understand that his theology was based on a powerful understanding of grace—prevenient, justifying, and sanctifying. He focused on grace so much that in all other matters of worship, church governance, modes of baptism, or theological explorations he advocated great tolerance. As noted in *The Book of Discipline*, Wesley stated, "As to all opinions which do not strike at the root of Christianity, we think and let think." What mattered most was simple: faith and love; grace embodied. Given our United Methodist heritage, formulating doctrine has been less pressing than calling people to faith and nurturing them in the knowledge and love of God (¶ 103).[8]

Alongside this, our theology carries a strong emphasis on disciplined and critical thinking. This becomes apparent as you examine and develop an understanding of United Methodism's theological task.

United Methodism's Theological Task

Simply stated, theology is our effort to articulate God's grace and action in our lives. In response to Christ redeeming us, our theological explorations seek to express the mysterious reality of God's presence, peace, and power in the world. In doing so, we hope to understand more clearly the encounter between the divine and the human. Such understanding prepares us to participate in God's work in the world with more clarity and energy.

The Christian tradition encourages serious reflection by all Christians across the spectrum of theological thinking. To that end, some important principles guide United Methodist theology. *The Book of Discipline* examines these principles in depth in the section *Our Theological Task* (¶ 105). The principles are highlighted below and merit further study by a careful reading of *The Book of Discipline*.

- **Our theological task is both critical and constructive.** We ask critical questions of faith expressions: Are they true? Clear? Credible? Are they based in love? Are they faithful to the gospel? We also ask constructive questions in order to renew our thinking about God, revelation, sin, redemption, justice, and other theological concerns. This constructive task summons us to understand the gospel in our own sometimes troubled and uncertain times.
- **Our theological task is both individual and communal.** As Christians we are to be individuals who hunger to understand the truth revealed in Jesus Christ. Scholars have their role in this endeavor, but all Christians are called to prayerful theological reflection. Our task is also communal. It happens in conversations open to the experience, insights, and traditions of all who make up United Methodism. This dialogue belongs to every congregation and campus ministry setting—members and visitors—and to all clergy—bishops, pastors, deacons, and elders—and to every agency and theological school of the Church.
- **Our theological task is contextual and incarnational.** God came to us in flesh and blood in a certain time and place; Jesus Christ embodied and involved in the world is the basis for our theological work. As Jesus embraced the world in his life, our theology must also energize us through our involvement in the world around us.

25

- **Our theological task is essentially practical.** Theology informs our everyday decisions as well as the Church's daily work. The truth of any theological statement is measured by its practical significance. Theology should clarify our thinking and affect what we say and do. It should help us integrate the gospel—its promises and its demands—into our daily lives.

General Rules and Their Use in Small Groups

Wesley's General Rules were originally designed for members of Methodist societies and rooted firmly in the principle of practicing the Gospel in daily life. These societies were small groups committed to living their faith with intention and purpose. These rules were simple for small group members to understand but not always easy to follow.

Wesley set out his expectations for those striving to "evidence their desire of salvation":

> **First:** By doing no harm, by avoiding evil of every kind . . .
> **Secondly:** By doing good . . . of every possible sort, and, as far as possible, to all . . .
> **Thirdly:** By attending upon all the ordinances of God [which included public worship, the ministry of the Word, Holy Communion, family and private prayer, searching the Scriptures, and fasting or abstinence] (¶ 104).

By these general rules Wesley urged group members to "watch over one another in love" in their daily discipleship. Their weekly meetings were an opportunity for prayer, reflection, and accountability. Through these rules, along with the higher rule of Scripture, God's Spirit "writes on truly awakened hearts." Wesley believed these were sufficient for both faith and practice, and United Methodists are still encouraged to practice these rules today.

Mission and Connectionalism

- **Faith and good works.** We believe faith and good works belong together. God calls forth in us a love of Christ that overflows into a love for all people. Wesley called people to actions borne out of a heart aflame with Christ's love. This kind of experience leads believers to gather in places where God is—among the broken in the world. To listen, minister, feed, heal, and challenge: these are some of the ways faith and works are made known in the world.

- **Mission and service.** We believe personal salvation always involves Christian mission and service. Personal religion, evangelical witness, and Christian social action are dynamically linked. Scriptural holiness gives rise to personal piety, but it does not stop there. Love of God always joins with love of neighbor and a passion for justice in the life of the world.

- **Connected for mission.** We believe all Christians are bound together closely, and the worshipping community nourishes the personal experience of faith. We believe the outreach of the church originates from the working of the Spirit, and in a church that works together, sharing insights and resources, and encouraging, challenging, and supporting one another. As United Methodists, we work through a connectional organization based on mutual support, responsibility, and accountability. Our connectional ties strengthen us to do God's work in the world, to join other faith communities in that work, and to be renewed to take up that calling every day.

Social Principles

The *Social Principles*, written in Part V of *The Book of Discipline* and Part I of *The Book of Resolutions of The United Methodist Church,*[9] represent the most recent summary of the Church's thought about our faith's impact on current social, economic, and political issues. The United Methodist Church discusses, updates, and reaffirms these at each General Conference. Opposition to human trafficking, slavery, inhumane prison conditions, child labor, and other concerns reflect our Church's commitment to human dignity and social reform. The United Methodist Church proclaims that there is no personal gospel that fails to express itself in social concerns. Likewise, there is no social gospel that does not include personal transformation. The moral and spiritual qualities of our society are intertwined, and we express these beliefs in the *Social Principles.*

Our Sources: Scripture, Tradition, Reason, and Experience

Wesley considered four sources key for making faith-based decisions. He believed the core of Christian faith is (a) revealed in Scripture, (b) illuminated by tradition, (c) made vivid in personal experience, and (d) confirmed by reason.

Of these, Scripture is primary and must be the focus of disciplined study. Tradition includes writings and thoughts ranging from early Christians to Protestant Reformers to ecumenical works to the literature of contemporary spirituality. The authority of tradition is measured by its faithfulness to the message of the Bible. The Christian witness is not fully understood unless individuals experience faith in their own lives. Experiencing God's presence, experiencing the working of the Spirit in the world, and making those experiences an integral part of life make faith powerful and vivid. Making sense of the Christian faith requires the use of reason. Common sense knowledge, education, and life experience all contribute to how Scripture is interpreted and guides our lives and the Church's ministry.

The interaction of these four, with Scripture as the primary authority, brings insight and imagination to a dialogue about faith and its substance in everyday life. Understanding the Bible and Christian history (both personal and held in common) enrich and challenge us to live our best Christian witness.

Our Theological Context

All of these—the Church's theological task, the General Rules, mission and connectionalism, the Social Principles, and our four sources—form the heritage and inheritance of United Methodism. As you consider your call to ministry, immerse yourself in this theological context. This richness is inherent to who we are as United Methodists. This challenge is also intensely personal and passionately social. Consider these prayerfully as you discern your call.

Reflections

Think about what you have read in the previous pages.
- How do these beliefs interface with your own?
- Which ones resonate with you the most? Why? Which ones do you resist? Why?
- Which ones give you pause?
- How do these principles support, challenge, or inspire you?
- What would a community guided by these principles look like? How would it feel to be part of this community?
- Learning is part of discernment. What beliefs/topics/practices of United Methodist theology do you need to learn more about as you discern God's call?

Resources

- *Ways of Being, Ways of Reading: Asian-American Biblical Interpretation*, edited by Mary F. Foskett and Jeffrey Kah-Jin Kuan: *Ways of Being, Ways of Reading* is a collection of essays on the role of the Bible and its interpretation from an Asian North perspective. A large handful of scholars contribute to this volume and address a variety of themes and topics from an Asian-American perspective. (Chalice Press, 2006)
- *Polity, Practice, and the Mission of The United Methodist Church*, by Thomas Edward Frank: Commissioned by the General Board of Higher Education and Ministry of The United Methodist Church for use in United Methodist history, doctrine, and polity courses, this in-depth analysis of the connection between United Methodist polity and theology addresses the ways historical developments have shaped—and continue

to shape—the organization of The United Methodist Church. This resource also includes updated denominational statistics, as well as references to recent works on The United Methodist Church and American religious life. (Abingdon Press, 2006)

- *Mañana: Christian Theology from a Hispanic Perspective,* by Justo L. González: In this work, González traces major theological conversations through a Hispanic perspective. Specifically focused on the Hispanic community, González unfolds larger Catholic and Protestant experiences in Hispanic religious communities as context for larger discussions around creation, reading the Bible in Spanish, the Reformation, ecumenism, and more. (Abingdon Press, 1990)
- *Three Simple Rules: A Wesleyan Way of Living,* by Rueben P. Job: A modern interpretation and simple but challenging look at John Wesley's General Rules: "Do no harm, do good, stay in love with God." (Abingdon Press, 2007)
- *Introduccíon a la vida y telogía de Juan Wesley,* by Hugo Magallanes: This Spanish resource examines the life and theology of John Wesley, as well as the relevance of Wesley to Hispanic people in the United States and Latin America. (Abingdon Press, 2005)
- *The Method of Our Mission: United Methodist Polity & Organization,* by Laceye Warner: This resource lays out four important aspects for understanding United Methodism—beliefs, mission, practice, and organization. This book was written specifically for courses on United Methodism and lends itself particularly well to anyone looking for a more didactic, structured

resource on the Church today and its Wesleyan roots. (Abingdon Press, 2014)

- *Toward a Feminist Wesleyan Theology*: A conversation between Wesleyan theology and feminist theology, this edition of the journal *Quarterly Review* published by the General Board of Higher Education and Ministry of The United Methodist Church examines the early sensibilities of the Wesleys toward women and their place in the culture. It considers the Wesley family women, theologians in their own right, and explores the interaction of the Methodist movement and the Woman movement of the nineteenth century. Access this resource at http://www.quarterlyreview.org/pdfs/vol23no4winter2003.pdf. (*Quarterly Review*, Winter 2003)
- *Class Leaders: Recovering a Tradition*, by David Lowes Watson: This book demonstrates how the Methodist movement effectively developed a structured leadership to nurture accountable discipleship. Wesley's adoption and promotion of the class system was essentially *ecclesiolae en ecclesia*, "little churches within the big church." (Wipf & Stock Publishing, 2002)
- Many of John Wesley's most important sermons have been collected by the General Board of Global Ministries of The United Methodist Church as a listing of titles with links to the full sermon. You can access these at http://www.umcmission.org/find-resources/john-wesley-sermons.
- *Sisters in the Wilderness: The Challenge of Womanist God-Talk, Anniversary Edition* by Delores S. Williams: In this landmark work, Williams offers African-American womanist theology by using the story of Hagar as the

foundation for a theological discussion on the experiences and struggles of African-American women. Touching on topics such as surrogacy, motherhood in the context of resistance, black liberation theology, and womanist-feminist dialogue, Williams's book pushes the reader to engage in theology from the perspective of African-American women today and through the centuries. (Orbis Books, 2013)

- *The Book of Discipline of The United Methodist Church:* Updated at General Conference every four years, *The Book of Discipline* is the book of laws by which United Methodists structure and govern themselves. This resource reflects what United Methodists believe about the Church, the ministry of clergy and laypersons, and United Methodism's mission in the world, as well as contains founding historical documents and beliefs from Methodism's inception. (United Methodist Publishing House, 2012)

- *The Book of Resolutions of the United Methodist Church:* Organized into seven sections—The Natural World, The Nurturing Community, The Social Community, The Economic Community, The Political Community, The World Community, and Other Resolutions—*The Book of Resolutions* sets the framework for how United Methodists apply the Church's beliefs to daily practice and current social issues. Similar to *The Book of Discipline, The Book of Resolutions* is updated every four years at General Conference. (United Methodist Publishing House, 2012)

Chapter Three
What United Methodists Believe:
Grace and the Sacraments

Grace comes as a gift. We can neither earn it nor make it happen.

—Gerald May[10]

You are loved, someone said. Take that and eat it.

—Mary Karr[11]

Grace: Prevenient, Justifying, and Sanctifying

For John Wesley and early Methodists, grace was the powerful process by which believers came to experience God and know God's salvation. Wesley believed grace was ever-present and influential in believers coming to repentance. He believed grace could lead believers to love God with all their being and to love neighbors and the world as they loved themselves.

Wesley understood God's grace as a unified piece, but for teaching he defined grace as having three aspects: prevenient, justifying, and sanctifying. The metaphor of a house can be helpful here: "[John Wesley] saw prevenient grace as the porch of the house, an entryway, that invites us to come further. Justifying grace is the door into the house. We must open it and come inside if we truly are to experience and know the whole house. Sanctifying grace is learning to live in and grow in the whole house."[12]

Prevenient Grace: The Grace That Surrounds Us

Prevenient grace is the grace that comes to us even before we know God—the porch before we enter the house. God showers it upon all people whether they are aware of it or not. Through prevenient grace, God takes the initiative in beginning a relationship with us. Prevenient grace is God's way of showing us that no matter who we are or where we are, God is already there ahead of us, waiting for us. God's prevenient grace precedes us wherever we go.

In his book *A Lover's Quarrel with the World*, Maurice Boyd writes of the celebrated British journalist and lay preacher Hugh Redwood. During a difficult time in his life, Redwood felt that no matter how earnestly he prayed he could not discern the guidance of the Lord.

One night, while sitting by the fire in the guest room where he was staying, he picked up the Bible on his night table. It was open to Psalm 59. Redwood began to read, and when he got to the tenth verse he found these words: "The God of my mercy shall prevent me."

Redwood read these words from the King James Version of the Bible. To the modern reader, prevent means "to keep something from happening." But in 1611, in King James English, prevent meant, "to go before." Today we would translate Psalm 59:10 as, "God will go before me" (NIV).

After reading that psalm, Redwood saw a note he would never forget; someone unknown to him had written in the margin, "My God, in . . . loving-kindness, shall meet me at every corner." These powerful words spoke to Redwood that night. God was there. God's grace preceded him to that place and waited for him there.[13] *for me!*

God preceding us, God going before us and waiting for us, God in loving-kindness meeting us at every corner: this is prevenient grace. This is the grace John Wesley believed is lavish and free and available to us all.

Justifying Grace: The Grace That Makes Our Brokenness Whole

Justifying grace brings a big change to the relationship we have with God—it's the door to the house, which we must open. Through justifying grace we begin to realize and trust (have faith) that we are restored to relationship with God. We come to acknowledge our sinfulness and trust that we are forgiven by God's grace. Just as justifying text in a document aligns it a certain way (e.g., right- or left-justified), justifying grace aligns us with God through Jesus Christ.

As noted in *The Book of Discipline*, justifying grace is when "God reaches out" to a person "with accepting and pardoning love." The moment of justification brings about a true personal change. This change includes feelings of peace, hope, and joy. Such an experience "may be sudden and dramatic, or gradual and cumulative. It marks a new beginning, yet it is part of an ongoing process" (¶ 102).

37

He was there even when I didn't know Him. He is always there!

To know God's love in this way, to be touched by God's justifying grace is a life-changing, life-rearranging experience. It creates in us an urgency to know God, to follow in God's way, and to trust that God is always with us. As poets and theologians often remind us, there are as many ways to realize and accept God's justifying grace as there are ways to fall in love. For some people, it happens all at once—"at first sight." For others, it is gradual and cumulative. Some people come to love eagerly; others need more time, fearing or resisting vulnerability.

The way you come to receive God's grace does not matter nearly as much as the truth of God reaching out to you with justifying grace and making you a new creature in Christ.

Sanctifying Grace: Smoothing Out the Rough Edges

Prevenient grace is God meeting you at every corner. Justifying grace is God reaching out to you with love. When you say yes to the invitation of justifying grace, you turn a corner in your faith journey. What comes next? Entering the house: living and growing in this new home.

One of the most controversial teachings of the early Methodist movement was that it is possible for us to realize Christian perfection in this life—perfect love, loving perfectly. Wesley called this process "going on to Christian perfection," or sanctifying grace. Sanctifying grace challenges believers to go deeper in the faith, to love the world more energetically, and to keep growing in the knowledge and love of God.

For Wesley, God's sanctifying grace led believers to have their hearts "habitually filled with the love of God and neighbor" (¶ 102). For you, this might mean coming to understand your life as more and more focused on living by faith. Faith becomes the center out of which you live. Little by lit-

38

tle, God's sanctifying grace uncovers more and more of God's image in you. As one who has been forgiven, you become more forgiving. As one who is loved, you become more loving. Wesley emphasized that as we are continually filled with God's love, we are led more fully to acts of mercy and works of justice.

Ralph Wood, Professor of Theology and Literature at Baylor University, describes grace as a "comedy of redemption." To illustrate the point, Wood refers to the fiction of Peter De Vries, "a writer so funny that it may seem inappropriate to take him seriously."[14]

Wood admires De Vries for his sense of humor: puns (Like the cleaning lady, we all come to dust.), aphorisms (What is an arsonist but someone who's failed to set the world on fire?), and malapropisms (A novel should have a beginning, a muddle, and an end.)—De Vries is master of all these and more. Yet time and again De Vries's characters, in their own bumbling ways and in spite of their pessimistic philosophies, testify to divine grace set firmly in the muddle of human existence. In De Vries's world, grace comes to these women and men more often than not despite their unbelief and lapses of faith. Maybe that is the way it is for us, too. Maybe God's grace negates our attempts to negate God's mercy.[15]

Perhaps we are so thoroughly surrounded by God's grace each day we fail to even recognize it. We are saved not by any effort of our own; there is no way to earn our salvation. We are saved by the unbidden grace of God, which is near to hand, overhead and underfoot, in the eyes of strangers and friends, heard as laughter sometimes and other times as tears.

Thank God for that.

The Sacraments: Signs of Grace

United Methodists affirm and practice two sacraments: baptism and Holy Communion. The sacraments are signs of God's grace and good will toward us. The sacraments strengthen and confirm us in the faith.

Baptism

Baptism is an event in which we touch, taste, feel, experience, and know the love of God. Through water at baptism we celebrate God's love for God's children. Baptism means God claims us as God's own. While some churches do not believe in baptism for infants, reserving baptism for people who make their own faith commitment, United Methodists believe baptism, as God's grace, is a gift from God. Therefore, there is never a time when one is old enough, smart enough, or good enough to deserve it.

All persons at any age and of any ability should be showered with the grace of God and the gift of baptism. Sprinkling, dipping, and full immersion—these are all ways of affirming God's gift of new birth and life for us. And through the individual's baptism, the community also shares in this sacrament by promising to support and pray for the person as she or he grows in faith and lives a life of discipleship.

Baptism is important to the individual + the content of the Church as well.

Holy Communion

Holy Communion is both a sign of the love Christians ought to have for one another and a demonstration of our redemption through Christ. With the bread we partake of the body of Christ; with the cup we partake of the blood of Christ. Through Holy Communion, Christ's life becomes part of our

40

lives. It is a time when we commune with other believers and with God.

While some churches have a "closed" communion, meaning they invite only members of their church or only those who are baptized to share in Holy Communion, The United Methodist Church celebrates "open" communion. "Christ our Lord invites to his table all who love him, who earnestly repent of their sin and seek to live in peace with one another."[16] For Wesley, Holy Communion was a means of grace whereby some are converted to the faith.

Blocking Communion (grace) may Blotth Conversion Faith.

Grace, Sacraments, and Community

Grace—prevenient, justifying, sanctifying—comes to each of us individually. But it also comes to us in community, both in worship and in other times that the community of Christians gathers together. We recognize God's grace in and through one another. We worship together and will often participate in the sacraments as a part of that worship time. The "great cloud of witnesses" is emboldened by grace—in community. Through baptism and Holy Communion, the community recognizes and names the grace that is in you and surrounds you.

In her award-winning novels about Armand Gamache, Chief Inspector in the Sûreté du Québec (Quebec's major police force), Louise Penny captures what it means to be a member of a caring, accountable community. Just four sentences, her protagonist says to his officers, are what matter most in their work and in their lives: "I'm sorry. I was wrong. I need help. I don't know."[17]

Four short sentences—a lifeline, a reminder. For us, it is a significant reminder about grace and community. Opening to God and to one another, knowing ourselves and being honest about that—this is where God's grace meets us. Here, in community, God's grace is always at hand.

Reflections

- Consider the three forms of grace as Wesley understood them. Identify times your own life has been touched by each of these aspects of grace—prevenient, justifying, and sanctifying.
- What does Psalm 59:10—the God of mercy shall go before me—mean to you and your faith?
- If, as Peter De Vries writes, grace is sometimes a comedy of redemption, can you remember a time when God's grace came to you as laughter, or from some unlikely or unexpected source?
- Discuss, in your own words, why United Methodists baptize infants and children.
- When you hear, "Remember your baptism and be thankful," what does that mean to you? When you receive communion, what does this mean to you? How will the sacraments shape you as a disciple?
- Are you surprised to learn that Wesley opened the table of Holy Communion to all—including non-believers? Why did he do this? Do you know of other traditions that practice this open table? There are traditions that practice a "closed table" for communion. Are you familiar with any of these? What is your personal response to these ideas about Holy Communion?
- Why are baptism and Holy Communion celebrated in community? How do the sacraments shape our Church as a community of faith?

- How do you envision the sacraments as a part of your ministry?

Resources

- *Living Our Beliefs: The United Methodist Way,* by Kenneth L. Carder: An engaging summary of the most critical elements of John Wesley's ideals, accompanied by ways those ideals can be put to use in today's world. Also contains an extensive bibliography. (Discipleship Resources, 2009)
- *Wesley, Aquinas, and Christian Perfection: An Ecumenical Dialogue,* by Edgardo Colón-Emeric: One of the most controversial teachings of the early Methodist movement is that it is possible for us to realize Christian perfection in this life; however, this was not the first or only time perfection became a focus in Christian theological reflections. In this book, Colón-Emeric sets John Wesley in conversation with Thomas Aquinas on the matter of Christian perfection—and finds that the gap between the two is not as wide as we might think. A great exercise in ecumenism, Colón-Emeric's book engages Catholics and Methodists who wish to know more about one another. (Baylor University Press, 2009)
- *Fiesta Cristiana: Recursos para la Adoración,* by Joel Martínez and Raquel Martínez: Written and compiled by retired United Methodist Bishop Joel Martínez and his wife, Raquel Martínez, *Fiesta Cristiana* offers a variety of United Methodist liturgies and services in both Spanish and English. From Easter and baptismal services to services and creeds from the Hispanic commu-

nity and hymns, this resource allows English-speaking and Spanish-speaking communities to celebrate and worship together. (Abingdon Press, 2003)

- *John Wesley's Sermons: An Anthology*, edited by Albert C. Outler and Richard Heitzenrater: Collected by these renowned Wesley scholars, this anthology contains 50 of Wesley's finest sermons, arranged chronologically with introductory commentary by Richard Heitzenrater. (Abingdon Press, 1991)
- "Cyber Disciples: A New Theological Subject and Online Communion," by HiRho Park: The 2012 General Conference, through the Committee on Faith & Order, authorized a study of online communion in order to develop a denominational understanding of offering communion via an online setting. Essays posted on this page contribute to the ongoing discussion regarding online communion. In this particular essay, Park asks larger questions of ecclesiology, and how the new ways United Methodists live out their faith in a fast-changing world affect the way we approach practices such as communion. (http://www.gbhem.org/about-gbhem/publications/online-communion, date accessed: June 10, 2015)
- "By Water and the Spirit: A United Methodist Understanding of Baptism": This report articulates The United Methodist Church's official understanding of holy baptism. To download the full text of "By Water and the Spirit," visit http://www.umcdiscipleship.org/resources/by-water-and-the-spirit-full-text.
- "This Holy Mystery: A United Methodist Understanding of Holy Communion": Similar to "By Water and the Spirit," this report articulates The United Methodist Church's

official understanding of Holy Communion. To download the full text of "This Holy Mystery," visit http://www.umcdiscipleship.org/resources/this-holy-mystery-a-united-methodist-understanding-of-holy-communion1.

Chapter Four
Spiritual Disciplines

Some days, although we cannot pray, a prayer
utters itself.

—Dame Carol Ann Duffy[18]

Growing and nurturing your faith, and finding it when it is mislaid—that is a challenge. It is scandalously easy to forget to rely on faith. When things are going well, faith can fade to the background. When things are going wrong, fear and pain can drown it out.

The practice of spiritual disciplines will sustain you through all of it. Spiritual disciplines are those practices that nourish your individual and communal faith. These disciplines will help you find your sometimes-mislaid faith, bring you closer to God, and give you the strength to be in holy community with others. Spiritual disciplines can, with practice, become the source of your greatest strength, your boldest courage, and your deepest quiet center.

Through the centuries, the church has taken a variety of approaches to spiritual disciplines. Each succeeding generation of believers experienced themselves and God in unique moments, and with their disciples uncovered many ways of staying close to God.

Wesley and Spiritual Disciplines

For John Wesley, spiritual disciplines were a means of grace to open oneself to God's presence and guidance. Wesley believed God accompanied believers in their spiritual journeys every day—in times of joy and celebration as well as in times of sorrow and mourning. For Wesley, spiritual disciplines provided the means to keep close to God and live as Jesus lived.

Wesley understood the spiritual disciplines as a means of grace, a way to help people cultivate lives of faith. He believed God did not abandon us on our spiritual journeys, but gave us disciplines to lead us into deeper relationship with God and with each other. Wesley divided these disciplines into two categories: acts of piety and acts of mercy.

Acts of piety focus on the practice of several disciplines: prayer, the study of Scripture, Holy Communion, fasting, and Christian conferencing. These tend the inner life of faith. Wesley practiced these disciplines faithfully no matter what the demands on his time—and those demands were great. He considered these spiritual disciplines to be critical to his life of preaching and witness.

Wesley addressed faith's outer life, the life of service, through acts of mercy. He taught that acts of mercy—such as caring for the poor, speaking out against slavery, living modestly, and showing kindness—are just as critical to the spiritual formation of the faithful. Works of mercy, he said, lead believers to experience the presence of God and to be conformed to a life based on the example and inspiration of Jesus.

The Rich Landscape of Spiritual Disciplines

Your Christian heritage contains centuries of communities seeking God in their daily lives, and these strong, deep, imaginative ways of life have much to offer in your own spiritual formation. There may be no better time to go deeper in your faith than when you're exploring your candidacy for ordained or licensed ministry. The enduring disciplines of solitude, silence, and Scripture practiced by generations of the faithful who have gone before you can be your lifelines.

Here is a brief look at a handful of spiritual disciplines. Several are traditional and have been passed down for centuries, while others are newer. Listen carefully to hear which disciplines speak to you; look for the ones God might be leading you to practice.

- **Lectio Divina.** Praying the Scripture in order to listen for what God is saying to you or to the community. You are not trying to memorize Scripture or analyze it—only to bring an open and expectant attitude to it.
- **Journaling.** Journaling in search of spiritual meaning is more than a recollection of daily events. Writing as a spiritual discipline helps you uncover the meaning behind what is happening to you, discover where you were present to God, and hear God's voice speaking within you.
- **Daily Prayer.** This is the simple, powerful act of being in touch with God. In prayer you praise God, ask for forgiveness, open yourself to God's companionship, intercede for others, and offer gratitude. You might use a visual symbol or music for focus during prayer, and you might pray in common with others or choose to

pray alone. Setting aside a daily time and a quiet place for prayer is an important part of this discipline.

- **Spiritual Reading.** Followed by time for reflection, spiritual reading can be rich and transformative. Whether you are reading a sermon, a book of prayers, a novel, a newspaper, or someone's blog, all of these can lead you deeper into the life of faith and the life of the world. The critical part of spiritual reading is the time you spend reflecting on what you have read and understanding where you are being challenged or led.

- **Confession.** Confessing our sins to others, such as a pastor or a trusted friend, can be an immense relief. Often what makes a sin so burdensome is not the guilt of having committed it, but the shame we expect to feel if our sin is found out—a feeling that can cause us to isolate ourselves from community. Consider making confession a regular practice with someone who can keep your confidences, and perhaps invite them to share their own. Being honest about your shortcomings in a purposeful, reconciliatory way can bring healing and lead you closer to God and others.

- **Spiritual Guide.** Another way God can speak to you is through a spiritual director. A spiritual director is someone with whom you share your spiritual struggles in order to gain wisdom or seek clarity. Spiritual directors also tend their own prayer and meditation, and their lives reflect trustworthiness and honesty. Through companionship with this person, you open yourself to the Holy Spirit for wisdom, encouragement, and discernment.

- **Simplicity.** The practice of simplicity is one of the oldest and most challenging spiritual disciplines, tracing its roots back to Jesus. In Luke 18:22, among other places in the New Testament, Jesus tells his followers, "Sell everything you own and distribute the money to the poor. Then you will have treasure in heaven. And come, follow me." Both inwardly and outwardly focused, this discipline calls for radical reliance upon God. But living simply, in the heart and in the world of possessions, brings with it the gift of focus. It fosters attention on what is important and frees up time and energy to spend on others. The practice of simplicity is neither materialism nor asceticism; it is what comes from seeking first the Kingdom of God.

Spiritual disciplines, spiritual practices, spiritual imagination, whether done in solitude or in community, are your lifelines to God. As you consider a life of tending the souls of others, take care to tend your own. A healthy practice of the spiritual disciplines forges a stronger bond between you and God—a source of great joy in life's celebrations and a rugged lifeline in times of brokenness. The time to build and strengthen your spiritual life is now. Tend your spirit. Care for your soul. Open yourself to God's great gifts.

Reflections

- Choose one new spiritual discipline to practice over the next month. Talk about your experience during this month. What word or phrase best describes your experience with this discipline? What was easiest about the practice? What was most difficult? Share your experience and insights with your mentor and/or your mentor group.

- Talk with two or three people in your church, your family, or your community about their spiritual lives. Find out what spiritual disciplines they practice, when they learned about that practice, and what difference it makes in their lives.
- Spiritual disciplines invite you to look more closely at yourself. Has practicing spiritual disciplines revealed things about you that surprise you? That cause you concern? That give you joy?
- Which spiritual discipline(s) do you think might sustain you in good times? Which might you turn to in times of trouble and unrest?

Resources

- *Qu4rtets*, by Jeremy Begbie, Makoto Fujimura, Bruce Herman, and Christopher Theofanidis: Inspired by T.S. Eliot's *Four Quartets*, artists Makoto Fujimura and Bruce Herman, along with composer Christopher Theofanidis and theologian Jeremy Begbie, began touring their exhibition, *Qu4rtets*, an artistic response to Eliot's work in word, image, and music. For more on the exhibit, visit http://fujimurainstitute.org/qu4rtets/ (date accessed: March 19, 2015).
- *Psalms: The Prayer Book of the Bible*, by Dietrich Bonhoeffer: In three brief chapters, Bonhoeffer captures a lifetime of prayer. Written in the 1930s during his years of imprisonment, this work recovered for him the practice of praying the psalms at a turning point in his life and was a spiritual resource for many other martyred Christians in Germany during World War

II. (Augsburg Fortress Press, first English-translation paperback, 1974)

- *The Gospel in Solentiname*, by Ernesto Cardenal: This work is a collection of dialogue among peasants in Solentiname, a remote group of islands in Lake Nicaragua. Reflecting on the gospel readings each Sunday, the dialogue recorded in this collection is a classic work of liberation theology, highlighting the incredible insights gained when the gospels are read through the lens of the poor and oppressed. (Orbis Books, 2010)
- *Pilgrim at Tinker Creek*, by Annie Dillard: Delving into relationships with God and nature, fostering self-awareness, and reflecting on the goodness and the badness of the world, Dillard writes about the difference between walking with and without a camera—in itself a good definition of a spiritual discipline. (Harper Perennial Modern Classic, 2007)
- *Four Quartets*, by T.S. Eliot: *Four Quartets* is a collection of four poems published individually over a six-year span. It conveys in beautiful and mysterious ways the depth of our longing for redemption. (Mariner Books, 1968)
- *A Strange Freedom: The Best of Howard Thurman on Religious Experience and Public Life*, edited by Walter Earl Fluker and Catherine Tumbler: Howard Thurman, renowned preacher, spiritual advisor to Martin Luther King, Jr. and others, and co-founder of the first interracially pastored, intercultural church in the United States, left behind an immense legacy of spiritual writings. This collection gathers some of his thoughts on how religious experience infused life with meaning,

on his struggle with violence in America, and on the difficult questions, "Will your life be barren or fruitful?" and "What is the importance of prayer?" (Beacon Press, 1998)

- *A Celebration of Discipline: The Path to Spiritual Growth*, by Richard Foster: Classic spiritual disciplines reclaimed for modern-day Christians. These include inward disciplines, such as prayer, fasting, and meditation; outward disciplines, such as simplicity, service, and solitude; and corporate disciplines, such as confession, worship, and celebration. (HarperSanFrancisco, Third Edition, 2002)

- *Jornadas de Fe: Selecciones de El Aposento Alto*, by Carmen Gaud: *Jornadas de Fe* is a collection of daily meditations, with meditations taken from *Guía de Meditaciones Diarias: El Aposento Alto*, as well as meditations written specifically for this book. Though the book was prepared keeping in mind those with visual impairments, anyone can use this resource to find quiet and calm in their daily life. (Upper Room Books, 2000)

- *Compassion: A Reflection on the Christian Life*, by Donald P. McNeill, Douglas A. Morrison, and Henri J.M. Nouwen: This provocative book of meditations asks what it means to be compassionate in a self-centered world. It raises the question of whether we can follow the example of Jesus Christ and enter into the suffering of others. It is written to be an inspiration to all who look for true intimacy with God and a deeper relationship with others. (Image, 2006)

- *Singing the Lord's Song in a New Land: Korean American Practices of Faith*, by Su Yon Pak, Unzu Lee, Jung Ha

Kim, and Myung Ji Cho: *Singing the Lord's Song* begins with a discussion of the social history of the Korean American Church in the United States and explores ministry in that context. The book then identifies eight key practices of the Korean American community, such as singing, keeping the Sabbath, fervent prayer, and piety. (Westminster John Knox Press, 2005)

Chapter Five
Vocation, Call, and Gifts

Our vocation is not a sphinx's riddle, which we must solve
in one guess or else perish.

—Thomas Merton[19]

If your dreams do not scare you, they are not big enough.

—President Ellen Johnson Sirleaf[20]

Vocation and Call

The word *vocation* comes from the Latin *vocare*, which means
"to name" or "call." This definition is probably familiar to
you. But it might surprise you to learn there are several other
interesting words also derived from *vocare*: evoke, invoke,
advocate, equivocal, unequivocal, convocation, vociferous.
They all bear the same root, but each contributes its own
slant. Our calls are evoked in us, we invoke God's presence,
we yearn for advocates, we find ourselves alternatively equivocal and unequivocal, and we can at times be quite vociferous
along the way. So do not be afraid to be loud, to ask for help,

to listen deeply to God, and to be energetically equivocal and energetically unequivocal—sometimes at the same time.

The Call from Scripture

God calls us to action—to put down our nets; climb down from the tree; pray for those who persecute us; love God and neighbor. It is, as it has been for many who have answered the call before, a beckoning in our lives to live according to the example of Christ and to serve our neighbor in all we do.

One of the Bible's most compelling calls is in Luke 19:

> Jesus entered Jericho and was passing through town. A man there named Zacchaeus, a ruler among tax collectors, was rich. He was trying to see who Jesus was, but, being a short man, he couldn't because of the crowd. So he ran ahead and climbed up a sycamore tree so he could see Jesus . . . When Jesus came to that spot, he looked up and said, "Zacchaeus, come down at once. I must stay in your home today." So Zacchaeus came down at once, happy to welcome Jesus. Everyone who saw this grumbled, saying, "He has gone to be the guest of a sinner." Zacchaeus stopped and said to the Lord, "Look, Lord, I give half of my possessions to the poor. And if I have cheated anyone, I repay them four times as much." Jesus said to him, "Today, salvation has come to this household."

Zacchaeus's call story reminds us of the many difficulties and joys that come with being called. As Jesus approached Jericho, Zacchaeus became separated from everyone else—he was too short, unable to see, and forced to climb a tree just to glimpse Jesus. Zacchaeus was a tax collector and a ruler among them. So when the crowd saw Jesus with Zacchaeus, they were quick to point out Zacchaeus's faults: "He is a sinner," they grumbled. But Jesus called Zacchaeus down from that tree, walked with him before that grumbling crowd, and affirmed Zacchaeus's call—and Zacchaeus followed.

Your call may come directly—and you may respond eagerly, like Zacchaeus did. Or it may come differently and you may respond differently. Your call may come as it did to Samuel while he tended to the aging Eli. Three times God called to Samuel and each time Samuel thought it was Eli calling. It was only when the call came the fourth time, after Eli helped Samuel know it was a call from God, that Samuel answered, "Speak. Your servant is listening." Like Zacchaeus you may feel like an outsider or have people in your life who only see your limitations or mistakes. Or, like Samuel, you may find that sharing your call with another person leads you to the encouragement and wisdom you needed in order to hear it. It took Elizabeth, after all, to confirm to Mary her call to give birth to Jesus.

In Scripture there are different calls in different circumstances to different ends. Throughout the mentoring process you will have the chance to reflect on many of these scriptural calls and the joys and struggles they produce. That reflection will affect your own call and what you understand it to be. *The Book of Discipline* outlines one way United Methodists can understand a call: God's call to you has been there from the very beginning of your life; it is transformed by the waters of your baptism; it continues to take shape throughout your life (¶ 220).

Wesley believed that a call has always been present and always will be. Wesley's call and ministry were profoundly affected by his upbringing. He was raised in a home that reflected the spiritual heritage of Puritanism, with its emphasis on discipline and personal religious affections, and Anglicanism, with its emphasis on the sacraments. When he was six years old, he was saved from a fire in the rectory in Epworth, his family's home. It was a dramatic event, and after this experience his mother and others saw him as providentially set apart for God. This life-shaping experience continued to undergird much of his faith and ministry.

Wesley's understanding of call is summed up in *Wesley's Historic Three Questions*. Wesley's three questions—about a candidate's grace, gifts, and fruit—were for those who understand themselves to be called to set-apart ministry. They are closely interrelated; each question connects to the other; we look at each in the context of the others. Handed down by Wesley, these are the same questions that frame interviews with candidates today in local church Pastor/Staff Parish Relations Committees and in district Committees:

(1) Do they know God as pardoning God? Have they the love of God abiding in them? Do they desire nothing but God? Are they holy in all manner of conversation?

(2) Have they gifts, as well as evidence of God's grace, for the work? Have they a clear, sound understanding; a right judgment in the things of God; a just conception of salvation by faith? Do they speak justly, readily, clearly?

(3) Have they fruit? Have any been truly convinced of sin and converted to God, and are believers edified by their service? (¶ 310.1)

The interviews with your church and district Committee rely on these so The United Methodist Church can be assured that those who present themselves as candidates for ordained and licensed ministry are truly called by God and can demonstrate an understanding of the Wesleyan tradition. These questions will be the focus of reflection and conversation in the next few weeks of mentoring. These will also be crucial when you write your call statement in preparation for your meeting with the district Committee.

As you struggle with your call, remember: Jesus also struggled with his. He had to discover who he was in relationship to God and what it was God intended him to do. The Holy Spirit led Jesus; the Holy Spirit will lead you, too. And remember, undergirding all of this—your reflections, your challenges, your insights, and your questions—is God's grace.

Gifts

Identifying gifts—and claiming them—begins and ends with asking questions creatively and listening carefully to the answers. Ask some questions about yourself and your gifts. What brings you joy or inspires you? Are there certain tasks, hobbies, or activities that bring you satisfaction? What energizes you and gives you life? What bores you or makes you feel emotionally drained? Think about how other people have shaped you and your gifts. For what accomplishments, values, or tasks are you most complimented, noticed, or rewarded? Have others voiced gifts or values they see in you that you also see in yourself—or, perhaps, that you do not see? Reflect on how the wider community responds to you and understands your gifts.

Where Gifts Begin

Your gifts come from the whole of who you are. Many factors influence the whole of who you are—family of origin, family of choice, friends, your age, race, sex, gender, religious experiences, and education. Consider these questions to identify who has shaped you and your understanding of your identity:

Strong faith in God, but little in me.

- **Family of origin.** How does the influence of those who raised you manifest itself in your gifts for ministry? In your decision to explore ministry? How have these influences been positive? Negative? What impact do your early years have on the way you understand family? On the ways you relate to families around you?

Rebekah
Bravery
Cyndy
Tommy
Page
Tony
Madison

- **Family of choice.** Sometimes there are people outside your family of origin whom you have chosen—or who have chosen you—to be part of a family. These relationships might have started when you were young, or they may have begun only in the last few years. How do these people influence your gifts for ministry, your calling, and your confidence in what you bring to ministry?

Rebekah and Her support!

- **Current family and primary relationships.** Consider the people who are most important to you now. How have they changed you? Have they identified gifts you did not fully realize you had? Single, married, divorced, widowed, re-married, in a serious relationship—no matter what your current status, you are shaped by these important people in your life. How do your decisions about ministry affect them? How do you include them in your discernment process? How do they affect your decision-making?

- **Community of support.** Think about and name the places where you currently find support. Are these strong and evident? Are they easy to access, or do you need to nurture these relationships more intentionally? What challenges will you encounter as you seek to build systems that will both nurture and hold you accountable?
- **Sex and gender.** Reflect on how your <u>sex or gender</u> might affect your opportunities, your ministry style, or your work with those you serve. How have you observed women and men in ministry in your church or conference? Have you observed differences in the reactions of clergy and laity in your conference to men or women in leadership roles? At this point, do you think your support comes more readily from one sex or gender than another? As a professional, how do you see yourself relating to female colleagues? To male colleagues?
- **Race and ethnicity.** Your race—along with your language and your cultural heritage—influences your gifts and your presence in ministry with others. Can you think of an instance in which your cultural heritage has been important for your ministry? How does your race or ethnicity influence your spiritual formation and identity? How does it contribute to the relationships you have with others? How does it affect the way others perceive you? What are some ways we take cultural norms for granted? Name places you will find community support and care for your ministry.
- **Body.** How we feel about our body—from our tonal quality to our posture to the ways we move our body through our daily lives—can positively or negatively

63

affect our experience of ministry. People communicate not only with speech, but also with hands and arms, facial expressions, posture, and presence. Are you at peace with your physical attributes? What, if you could, would you change? Do you feel too young or too old to enter ministry? How do you experience others perceiving you, and what do you hope they perceive? Everyone has physical limitations; how will yours affect your ministry? What positive impact do they have? In what ways do our bodies extend beyond us? Some may baptize differently, or preside over communion differently. How can our differences be an opportunity for a congregation to understand something new?

- **Socioeconomic background.** Your socioeconomic background includes where you grew up, income level, occupation, family and collective values, and status. How does this background influence your spiritual formation and identity? How might this be helpful to you in ministry? How might it hinder? Is your socioeconomic background something you are comfortable revealing to others? Why or why not?

Triumph and Shortfall: Valuing Others' Perspectives

It has been said that if you want someone to get to know you, share three personal or professional triumphs with that person. If you want someone to get to know you better, share three of your shortfalls or failures.

This stands true also in discovering who you might be in ministry. An honest look at what you have accomplished and what that says about your gifts is an important and intriguing part of your discernment process. An honest look at where you have fallen short, failed, or come up empty is also important and intriguing. But the most revealing part of this examination comes when you share it with others and listen for their feedback.

Your candidacy mentor and group can gift you with life-changing critique and support *if* you gift them with honesty about yourself. Share with them a time when you felt successful and proud of something you accomplished professionally. Share a time when you failed and felt miserable about your effort. Share about a time when your experiences in church or other leadership positions affirmed, strengthened, or challenged your call. Listen carefully to the group's feedback. Focus your energy on what they say about your gifts. Focus also on their comments about where you lack skill, your areas of weakness, and the places you need to grow.

Identify other people in your life who will give you both accurate and supportive information about your abilities and performance. Ask five people—a family member, friend, co-worker, church member, clergyperson, classmate, colleague, professor, coach, or teammate—to share what they identify as your greatest gifts. Ask them to name what they see as areas in which you need to grow. What did you learn about yourself from these people? How can you grow from and nurture these insights?

Regard their information carefully. Use it to guide you in understanding your gifts and identifying areas in which you need help. Be bold as you claim your gifts; name the challenges you face. It will take courage to look at yourself honestly. It will take even more courage to show yourself honestly to others. Self-awareness and vulnerability are invaluable as you discern who you are and what you are called to do. Dive into this chance to let God speak to you in new ways.

Reflections

- What thoughts and feelings does the Scripture passage about Zacchaeus's call evoke in you? What do you make of the crowd's judgment of Zacchaeus and of Jesus calling him? Have you met that kind of reaction when you have told others you may feel called to licensed or ordained ministry? Zacchaeus was literally up a tree, trying to see Jesus. Do you think he was surprised when Jesus spotted him there and called him to come down? Is there a figurative tree in your life—one in which you may be hiding or one from which you watch for Jesus passing by?

- Consider the call narratives in this chapter, and research others in the Bible. With which calling do you most identify? Which seems most foreign to you? Do you relate to more than one of these stories? If so, which ones?

- Look over Wesley's three historic questions. Reflect on these and share your answers with your group. How are your responses similar to other responses? How are they different?

- What did you learn about yourself as you reflected on your own gifts? Were there surprises? Events or people you had forgotten about who influenced you? How do your answers shape your understanding of your call?

- The section "Where Gifts Begin" lists several critical influences on you—family, relationships, community, sex, gender, race, ethnicity, your body, and socioeconomic background. Talk with your mentor and your candidacy group about some of these. Which have most influenced the development of your gifts? Which have had the most positive impact on your gifts? Which get in the way of you claiming your gifts? Take special care to look at influences of which you may not have been as aware and consider some of the questions under each category above.

- With your group, go through the questions under "Triumph and Shortfall" on page 64. Again, be as open as you can in this discussion. Your mentor and group will most likely have interesting, if not impactful, feedback.

Resources

- *Practicing Our Faith: A Way of Life for a Searching People*, edited by Dorothy C. Bass: A down-to-earth, accessible work that takes twelve spiritual practices out of theory and into everyday life. She and a broad range of other writers make the connection between what Christians do and what they believe. (Jossey-Bass, second edition, 2010)
- *A Sacred Voice Is Calling: Personal Vocation and Social Conscience*, by John Neafsey: The author, a lecturer at Loyola University Chicago, writes about distinguishing between authentic callings and the competing culture's calls to power or money. Drawing on the wisdom of saints and writers through the ages, he makes the case for finding balance between listening to our hearts and listening with our hearts to the needs of the world. (Orbis Books, 2006)
- *Callings: Twenty Centuries of Christian Wisdom on Vocation*, by William Placher: Extensive collection of

primary source writings about callings from the Early Church, to the Middle Ages, the Reformation, and the Post-Christian World (1800 to present). Augustine, Christine de Pisan, Thomas a Kempis, Teresa of Avila, John Wesley, Simone Weil, Dorothy Sayers, and Thomas Merton are among those quoted. (William B. Eerdmans Publishing Co., 2005)

- *Answering Your Call: A Guide for Living Your Deepest Purpose*, by John P. Schuster: A corporate consultant and director of the leadership center at a Jesuit university, he asks very concrete questions on leading a called life and creating spirited workshops. (Berrett-Koehler Publishers, 2002)

- *Explore Calling:* Each person feels God's call in a different way: during communion, a mission trip, or in everyday activities and conversations. However the invitation comes, you must decide how to answer, and www.explorecalling.org provides resources to help you on the journey.

- *Forum for Theological Exploration:* FTE provides resources, events, networks, grants, and fellowships to cultivate tomorrow's leaders, pastors, and theological educators. FTE also provides a forum through which students, young adults, and partners explore their passion, purpose, and call. Resources include a guide to theological education, articles and books about vocation, and sound clips and interviews with current religious leaders. Visit their website at www.fteleaders.org.

Chapter Six
Same Spirit, Many Callings

The pitcher cries for water to carry
and a person for work that is real.

—Marge Piercy[21]

The place God calls you to is the place where your deep
gladness and the world's deep hunger meet.

—Frederick Buechner[22]

Beginning in Genesis with Adam and Eve tending the garden and continuing all the way through the Bible, God bestows on us the gift of work. "Work," says the poet Kahlil Gibran, "is love made visible."[23]

New dimensions to questions you have about work— your life's work, your daily work, work the Spirit may be calling you to do—can be revealed in new ways when you begin exploring work as a path to God. Work has both an external and an internal character. Its external character is made up of acquiring tools, skills, and knowledge. Its internal character is that of creativity and inventiveness.

The daily-ness of work is precisely the place where an intentional Christian lives out her or his vocation. There is a big difference between trying to bring God to your work and seeing God already at work there. This distinction is worth remembering as you discern where God is calling you next; the work you are doing right now is sacred work, and God is already with you in your workplace, no matter what the future brings.

Many people labor under the impression that those who work for the church—missionaries, certified lay ministers, licensed or ordained clergy—have a higher calling than those who work in other professions and jobs. There is very little in the Bible to support this understanding. For example, Luke 10:38–42, when Jesus visits Mary and Martha, is a text often used as a society-wide principle to value the contemplative (Mary-like) practice of poverty, chastity, and obedience to the church over the active (Martha-like) life of secular work, family, and tending society.

But when this story from Luke is seen in its larger literary context (the story of the Good Samaritan—a true action story—comes just before), it is clear Jesus is not saying that the life of contemplation is preferred over the life of action. Instead, Jesus is teaching that both action and contemplation are critical to the life of the faithful. The United Methodist Church affirms that God calls all people and that the work of the laity is as equally valuable as that of the licensed or ordained. God calls people both to church-related and to non-church-related work, and neither is superior to the other.[24]

There are many biblical examples of calls to church-related work. In Exodus, Miriam, a prophetess, leads God's people in worship after Pharaoh's army was destroyed in the Red Sea. In Mark, Simon and Andrew are called from fishing to supporting Jesus's work and evangelizing. In Acts, Barnabas, Saul, and John are called to proclaim the word of God in synagogues.

There are also many examples in the Bible of God calling people to non-church-related work. In Deuteronomy, Joshua is called to be a military and political leader. In Samuel, David is called to become king in the midst of a deep crisis in Israel. God calls Queen Esther to be an uninvited spokeswoman to the king, risking her life to save her people. In Acts, Lydia, a dealer in purple cloth, is called to provide financial support to the new church in Philippi.

Ecclesiastes makes a strong statement affirming many kinds of work as full-time service: "Whatever you are capable of doing, do with all your might." (9:10). If that statement seems strange, it is because the distortion—full-time Christian service equals church work—has been out there for so long. Are deacons, elders, and local pastors in full-time Christian service? Yes, they are. Are teachers, farm workers, parents, accountants, and day-care providers in full-time Christian service? Yes, they are. The call to follow Christ is at the root of every calling.

Christian service embraces everything done to make the world more what God intends it to be. As noted in Colossians: compassion, kindness, humility, gentleness, and patience are part of God's work, and part of yours (3:12). Keep in your mind and heart that, whatever your profession—whether it was something you did or did not have a choice in—the calling is to full-time service.

Deacons, Elders, and Local Pastors: Who They Are and What They Do

The distinctions among these ways to serve—as a deacon, elder, or local pastor—come from The United Methodist Church's long tradition and history of calling the faithful to service in the world and in the church. The Church understands that ordained and licensed ministers offer themselves to serve as "set-apart ministers" in ways that are different than laity (¶ 301). Over the centuries these roles have come into existence, been re-shaped by time and circumstance, and evolved into their present form. Consider the differences among these three ways of serving. Think about whether any one—or none—of these might become the way you respond to God's call.

Deacons

Deacons are called by God and authorized by The United Methodist Church. They are ordained by a bishop to a ministry of *Word, Service, Compassion, and Justice.* Deacons work in both the community and the congregation through a ministry that connects the two. Deacons live out Christian discipleship and create opportunities for others to enter into that discipleship.

Deacons serve and equip others to strive for justice, to serve the needy, neglected, and marginalized with compassion. Deacons teach and proclaim the Word. In the liturgy they assist elders with the sacraments of baptism and Holy Communion. They conduct marriages and funerals. They lead the congregation's mission to respond to the needs, concerns, and hopes of the world. At times, for the sake of extending the mission and ministry of the church, a bishop may grant a deacon the authority to preside at the sacraments of baptism and Holy Communion in the deacon's primary appointment.

Deacons may be appointed by a bishop to serve in a variety of settings. A few of these include:

- United Methodist-related agencies, educational settings (schools, colleges, theological schools), and general church agencies
- a local congregation or charge (music ministry, Christian education, mission outreach, youth ministry, business administration, evangelism, ethnic ministries)
- a cooperative parish (legal assistant, parish nurse)
- annual conference (connectional ministries, collegiate ministry, social justice, mission strategy)
- agencies (community centers, aged-care facilities, counseling, hospice, hospitals, prisons, group homes)
- a district or group of churches (disaster relief, homeless ministry, community outreach, unemployment ministry, rehabilitation programs)

Deacons must have a high school diploma or equivalent, a Bachelor's degree (some exceptions apply), and a graduate degree. Options for the graduate degree include a Master of Divinity degree from a school of theology approved by The United Methodist Church's University Senate, or a master's degree in a specialized area plus the completion of the Basic Graduate Theological Studies. An alternative education route for candidates over 35 years old is the completion of a Bachelor's degree, professional certification, and Basic Graduate Theological Studies.

After completing at least half of the educational requirements, and upon receiving approval from the annual conference clergy session, a candidate may be elected to provisional membership and commissioned by a bishop. After completing the requirements of provisional membership, a candidate may apply to the conference Board of Ordained Ministry for recommendation for ordination and full membership. Following the Board's recommendation and approval by the clergy session, candidates for deacon are received into full membership and ordained by a bishop.

Deacons are clergy members of their annual conference, with full rights of voice and vote in the clergy session and annual conference. They serve and hold office as clergy on boards, commissions, or committees of the annual conference, and are eligible for election as clergy delegates to the general, central, or jurisdictional conferences.

Life as a Deacon

Deacons, with their specialized leadership skills, serve in a variety of settings and ways. Deacons may be teachers, community organizers, lawyers, doctors, administrators, youth ministers, campus ministers, scholars, advocates, or children's ministers. They may work in hospitals, nursing homes, corporations or businesses, private or public schools. One way to look at the ways deacons serve is to look briefly at the work and lives of several deacons carrying out their ministries.

Some deacons work in the local church. Jessie Waddell Teegarden, a provisional deacon in the Arkansas Conference, is director of early childhood and elementary ministries at Christ United Methodist Church in Memphis, Tennessee. She is also appointed to the Shelby County Schools in the Memphis area. "I think of myself as someone who is answering God's call to share God's love with children, to empower them through education so they might live into their identity as children of God," Teegarden affirms.

As a deacon who works as a Registered Nurse at a faith-based health organization and as a Clinical Health Partner with a local church, Marie King understands her ministry to be one of sacred trust. "When people realize you genuinely care and see that you are passionate about your calling they feel comfortable and trust you. I work with people during some of the most vulnerable times in their lives. Being a witness for Christ, being the hands and feet of Jesus, being a ministry of presence while providing health care ministry helps realize the connection between health and spirituality. In my work, I understand myself to be in ministry to and with the whole-person. I don't just focus on a single facet of an individual's health or life," King says.

Darren Hensley is an attorney in bankruptcy court. His presence as a deacon, he says, is a reminder to people that God is present with them in their time of financial vulnerability and crisis. His ministry is an "in-between" ministry. That is the image he uses to describe his life as it goes back and forth between the church gathered and the church sent. The support he gives is both legal and spiritual.[25]

DeAndre Johnson serves as the Minister of Music and Worship at Westbury United Methodist Church, in Houston, Texas. There are around 20 different nationalities represented in Westbury UMC's congregation—from regions such as the Caribbean, Central Africa, Southeast Asia, Europe, and North America. "As minister of music and worship, my role is to lead the congregation's worship and music ministries in ways that celebrate and nurture its multicultural identity," says Johnson, "while, at the same time, challenging and pushing [the congregation] toward the hard work of reconciliation and justice for our neighbors, both local and global."

"As a deacon," Johnson continues, "called to be that bridge between the worship life of the congregation and the needs of the world, I find great joy in helping people 'get it'—that is, helping people understand why we do what we do. It is amazing when they start to connect the dots in understanding how the faith they proclaim on Sunday is connected to the way they live on Wednesday. It is even more amazing when the songs we sing from different parts of the world begin to shape an individual's way of thinking about the world."

Gary Frieze works with people recovering from addiction. As a deacon, he helps the church focus on the needs of these people. At the same time, he brings the gospel to his addiction recovery work. The image he has for his ministry is that of being a bridge between the addictions clinic and the church. In that sense, he lays the needs of the world before the church and also ushers the church back out into the world.[26]

These are only a few of the settings in which deacons serve. Their ministries are as varied as the needs of the church, the needs of the world, and the gifts each deacon brings.

Elders

Elders are called by God and authorized by the church. They are ordained by a bishop to a ministry of *Word, Sacrament, Order, and Service.* Elders preach and teach the Word of God, provide pastoral care and counsel, administer the sacraments of baptism and Holy Communion, and order the life of the church for service in mission and ministry. The servant leadership of the elder, in both congregational and extension ministries, is expressed by leading the people of God in worship and prayer, leading people to faith in Jesus Christ, exercising pastoral supervision, and ordering the Church in mission in the world.

Elders serve as church pastors, but may also serve in extension ministries such as collegiate ministry, prison and hospital chaplaincy, or as professors in higher education and seminaries. Wherever elders serve, they carry their ordination to *Word, Sacrament, Order, and Service* as representatives of Christ.

For more than 200 years, elders in the Methodist tradition have agreed to offer themselves "without reserve to be appointed and to serve" for the sake of the mission of the church. The elder makes a commitment to full-time service and agrees to serve wherever the bishop appoints.

The majority of elders serve in local churches as pastors. The elder oversees the ministry of the church in its nurturing ministries, and in fulfilling its mission of witness and service in the world. This includes administrative oversight, evangelistic leadership, and disciple formation. Spiritual nurture and pastoral care in the congregation are central to elder ministry, as is setting the vision and direction of the congregation for its witness in the world. Elders lead the church in its worship and liturgical life.

Elders must have a high school diploma (or equivalent), a Bachelor's degree (a few exceptions apply), and a Master of Divinity degree from a school of theology approved by The United Methodist Church's University Senate. Or, an alternative educational route for local pastors over forty years of age is to complete Basic and Advanced Course of Study, and to serve a minimum of four years before applying for provisional membership. In addition, a health certificate, background checks, a written theological exam, an autobiographical state-ment, and a provisional period of service are required before a candidate is ordained elder.

After completing at least one-half of the Master of Divin-ity degree, and upon receiving approval from the annual conference clergy session, a candidate may be elected to pro-visional membership and commissioned by a bishop. After completing the requirements of provisional membership, a candidate may apply to the conference Board of Ordained Ministry for recommendation for ordination and full mem-bership. Following the Board's recommendation and approval by the clergy session, candidates for elder are received into full membership and ordained by a bishop.

Elders are clergy members of their annual conference, with full rights of voice and vote in the clergy session and annual conference. They serve and hold office as clergy on boards, commissions, or committees of the annual confer-ence, and are eligible for election as clergy delegates to the general, central, or jurisdictional conferences.

Life as an Elder

There are as many different stories about what it means to be an elder as there are elders in The United Methodist Church. Here, several elders in different ministry settings witness to their work and their daily lives.

"Preparing Sunday worship, visiting with people in the community who are suffering, weak, shut in or lonely, work-ing to maintain my own spiritual disciplines and habits—these are a few of the things I do each week as pastor of a local church in Virginia," says Taylor Mertins, a provisional elder in the Virginia Conference.

"As a young pastor in a church with predominately older members, I sometimes find myself challenged to make friends, inside or outside the congregation. Even so, being a pastor is the greatest job in the world. It has its challenges, but it is also incredibly rewarding. What other job would let me spend time deep in God's word to teach and preach, or let me preside over something as precious as water dripping over a child's head in baptism, or offering the [gift] of [Communion] to weary travelers of faith? What calling would give me the privilege of proclaiming God's presence in the midst of the suffering at a funeral, or in the joy of a wedding? It is a blessing to serve as a pastor, and more rewarding than I could have ever imagined," Mertins says.

Lieutenant Colonel Karen Meeker, an elder in the Susquehanna Conference, is a chaplain for the U.S. Army's 1st Armored Division stationed at Fort Bliss in El Paso, Texas. "As the Division Chaplain, I am responsible for the religious services and needs of the 19,000 soldiers who make up the Division, as well as their families. There are 45 chaplains and 45 chaplain assistants who minister to these people. I advise the Commanding General on the spiritual needs of the division and the post, which is comprised of 34,000 soldiers, nine chapel facilities, and over twenty chapel services," says Chaplain (LTC) Meeker.

"The hardest part of this ministry is going into a home to deliver the news that a loved one has died in combat. Knowing the news will forever change the lives of those I am going to see, I go praying to be a vessel of the Holy Spirit to comfort the grieving. . . . The United Methodist Church has sent me to proclaim the Good News of Jesus Christ and to offer the sacraments to our soldiers no matter where in this world they are deployed. It is an honor to represent the church in the U.S. Army," Meeker reflects.

Grace Community United Methodist Church is a diverse, passionate, and missional congregation in a suburban area of Shreveport, Louisiana. "I love preaching," reflects Juan Huertas, an elder in the Louisiana Conference and lead pastor at Grace Community, "love the challenge of leading in this season when the church is seeking to find once again its missional roots. I also love the opportunity to lead the staff from being doers of ministry to empowering God's people [at] Grace Community."

"I'm what I like to call a 'horizon pointer'—I see my role as one who points toward the vision of God's kingdom that is bubbling up around us," reflects Huertas. "It is exciting to continually point to the horizon, where our fruitfulness is rooted in becoming a community of conversation across the many things that divide us, one that incubates new ways of shaping disciples, and is constantly learning new ways of speaking and modeling the reality of the gospel to people who have never been connected to a congregation or who have left it."

Jenny Smith serves as an associate pastor at St. John United Methodist Church in Anchorage, Alaska. "It's an intriguing place to be in ministry," says Smith, "with high transiency rates, domestic violence [rates], and a deep sense of adventure and isolation. . . . It's a challenge to connect with so many diverse groups." Smith continues, "I am becoming a more whole person in Jesus as I learn from the experiences of my community. It's an honor to be invited into people's deep life moments—like weddings, funerals, and life transitions. To be given an opportunity to help name our deepest longings in connection with the good news of Jesus is a holy privilege."

Rev. Jay Williams, an elder in the New York Conference, currently serves in New England as lead pastor of Union United Methodist Church (Boston). "I love my job. I often say to myself, 'Wow, I get paid to do this!'" Williams reflects. "Hands-down, my favorite part of ordained ministry is creating space for people to encounter God dynamically. It gives me great joy to shape sanctuary, a place where both long-time churchgoers and those turned off by religion can experience God's presence. I love inviting people to the Table, inviting newcomers to faith through baptism, and inviting the entire gathered community to renewed life through the Sacraments."

Local Pastors

A local pastor answers God's call through serving a local congregation of The United Methodist Church. The local pastor performs the usual duties of a pastor including:
- preaching and teaching
- leading in worship and liturgy
- receiving new members
- presiding at the sacraments of baptism and Holy Communion as well as the services of confirmation and burial (in the specific congregation only)
- officiating marriage services (where state laws allow)

The local pastor's authority in these areas is within the specific appointment setting and does not extend beyond it. The local pastor is not ordained and serves under the authority of a license for pastoral ministry.

Local pastors oversee the ministry of the congregation where appointed to fulfill its mission of witness and service in the world. They provide pastoral support and guidance, and train lay leadership in fulfilling their ministries. Local pastors have administrative oversight of the congregation and supervise its programs.

Local Pastors are clergy members of the annual conference and are supervised by a district superintendent and bishop. They have limited voting authority, which is based on years of service and level of education completed. Local Pastors meet regularly with a clergy mentor and the district Committee on Ordained Ministry for ongoing approval to serve. Most of the time local pastors receive theological education through annual participation in the Course of Study. After completing the Course of Study, local pastors may enroll in the Advanced Course of Study or in another form of continuing education. Local pastors may also receive a Master of Divinity and continue to serve as a local pastor after the completion of that degree.

Students enrolled in theological studies in a college, university, or school of theology approved by the University Senate may also be appointed to serve as a local pastor in either the annual conference where their certified candidacy is held or in the annual conference where they attend school.

Educational requirements for local pastors include a high school diploma (or equivalent), completion of licensing school (to receive a License for Pastoral Ministry), and Basic Course of Study (a prescribed theological education course for local pastors). Advanced Course of Study (32 semester hours of graduate theological study) may be taken after completing Basic Course of Study. The License for Pastoral Ministry must be renewed annually.

Upon completion of the Basic Course of Study and meeting additional requirements, local pastors may also apply for Associate Membership in an annual conference. After completing the Advanced Course of Study and meeting additional requirements, local pastors or associate members may apply for provisional membership leading to ordination.

Associate Members are part of the itinerant ministry in the annual conference. They are available for appointment by a bishop, offering themselves without reserve. Associate members have the right to vote in all annual conference matters, except for constitutional amendments and matters of ordination, character, and conference relationship. They may serve on any board, committee, or commission of the annual conference. They may not be elected to general, central, or jurisdictional conferences; however, they may elect delegates.

Life as a Local Pastor

Mary Hatley, a local pastor, is assistant pastor at Cold Springs United Methodist Church in Concord, North Carolina. "I work with youth, children, and music. I also visit in the homes of church members who are sick or unable to get out. I love my work. The most challenging part of my ministry is translating what I see and feel about God into actions, activities, and events that help others grow in their witness and walk with God," says Hatley.

Just a "stone's throw" from the U.S.-Mexico border, in the Rio Grande Valley, is Valley Praise United Methodist Church in Harlingen, Texas, a satellite of First United Methodist Church Harlingen. "Harlingen is a community made up of roughly 80% Hispanics, mostly 2nd to 4th generation Americans of Mexican descent," says Aaron Saenz, a local pastor serving at Valley Praise. "We are a community transitioning from a rural farming community to a growing city with new economic development," Saenz says.

"What I love about being a local pastor is that I was able to jump feet first into ministry at a young age. I was not aware of this avenue of ministry growing up in the UMC, but it has afforded me an opportunity of a lifetime. . . . I feel that serving as a local pastor has allowed me to stay connected and grounded to my mission field. My theological education has come by way of Course of Study . . . and it has been of great benefit to me and my congregation. I was able to study and learn all while being in ongoing and exciting ministry," reflects Saenz. "In a time when we must stay connected and grounded to our mission fields in order to reach [people], the local pastor route enables us to remain relevant."

Susie Horner is a local pastor at Wakulla United Methodist Church in Florida. "Out of all the experiences I have had in my life, this . . . is the place I feel completed and happy," asserts Susie. "But don't think that as I began to discern my call that I welcomed it with open arms . . . because I didn't. I tried to run as fast as I could in the opposite direction. And it was when I began to run away that I began to experience God's love and grace. I finally realized I didn't want to run any longer, and since then I have seen how God uses my mistakes and bad decisions in the service of others on their own spiritual paths."

One Spirit, Many Callings: Taking It All into Account

The scope of ministry as a layperson in the work world, or as a deacon, elder, or local pastor seems almost limitless. Answering your call, striking out in any of these directions, finding your own particular way requires thought, prayer, reflection, deliberation, and vision. Your mentor and your candidacy group will continue to be pivotal in your process.

Consider your own gifts, circumstances, and understanding of what being at work in the world as a layperson, elder, deacon, or local pastor might mean for you. Imagine yourself on each of these paths—what might your work look like as a deacon? As an elder? As a faithful Christian in a setting outside traditional ordained or licensed ministry? What appeals to you about each of these? What gives you pause? To which form of ministry are you most attracted? Why? Which is least enticing? Why? Which feels as though it might fit you well? Which do you least envision yourself doing?

For people of faith, work is a path that can honor God and honors the gifts God has given you. As you walk farther along this path, know that God accompanies you and leads you each step of the way. Paul's letter to the Romans reminds us that each Christian has "different gifts" (12:6). Be ever mindful that your own particular gifts provide a vital contribution for the work of the whole community and for the redemption of the world.

Reflections

- "Many people labor under the impression that those who work for the church—missionaries, certified lay ministers, licensed or ordained clergy—have a higher calling than those who work in other professions and jobs. There is very little in the Bible to support this understanding." Reflect on this statement from the first part of this chapter. Do you know people who think being licensed or ordained is a higher calling than "regular" work? What were you taught about this as you were growing up? What do you believe about "secular" versus "sacred" work?

- The heart of this chapter contends that Christian service "embraces everything done" to make the world more whole, more the way God intends the world to be. How does this affect your understanding of your call? What does it mean for you to use this as a measure for your work? Can you articulate clearly how your call embodies Christian service that can help heal the world?

- Do you know people who have had little choice about what they do for a living? As an elder, deacon, or local pastor, how would you help talk with them about discernment and understanding their own call?

- Talk with a deacon, elder, or local pastor who is currently serving in ministry. Find out what they like about their work, what gives them pause, what they like least. Find out what daily life in their role and setting looks like. How do they address needs such as spiritual formation, peer support, continuing education? How would they characterize the balance (or imbalance) between work and personal life? What advice would they give to someone considering the form of ministry in which they work? If you are interested in more than one form of ministry, you may want to interview different people. If you need help identifying people to interview, your mentor can help you. Bring what you have learned back to your mentor and candidacy group for sharing and discussion.

Resources

- *The United Methodist Deacon: Ordained to Word, Service, Compassion, and Justice*, by Margaret Ann Crain: Clear descriptions of the identity and role of deacons, along with rich stories representing the variety of ministries to which deacons are called, make this book a compelling resource for those who are considering ministry as a deacon, as well as those who wish to gain a deeper understanding of the role. (Abingdon Press, 2014)
- *Ordained Ministry in The United Methodist Church*, by William B. Lawrence: Dean Lawrence of Southern Methodist University Perkins School of Theology in Texas works from the premise that, since Methodism began, Methodists have been trying to answer the question, "What is ordained ministry?" He begins with Wesley's eighteenth-century spiritual renewal (in the Church of England) and traces the question through to a Methodist Church of 70 million throughout the world. (General Board of Higher Education and Ministry of The United Methodist Church, 2011)
- *Extension Ministers: Mr. Wesley's True Heirs*, by Russell E. Richey: A United Methodist historian, Richey analyzes the evolving marginalization of "extension ministers" (United Methodist clergypersons serving the denomination in ministry settings beyond the local parish). Drawing on denominational history, theological argument, and practical experience, Richey offers insights for reintegrating this ministry into the United Methodist connectional covenant today. (General Board of Higher Education and Ministry of The United Methodist Church, 2008)

- *Formation for Ministry in American Methodism: Twenty-first Century Challenges and Two Centuries of Problem-Solving,* by Russell E. Richey: Another great resource by Richey, this work provides a critical analysis of the potential future of formation for ministry in the digital age. Richey also takes a look at how American Methodism has identified and formed its ministers since the late eighteenth century. (General Board of Higher Education of The United Methodist Church, 2014).
- *The Book of Discipline (2012)* includes descriptions, responsibilities, and requirements for all those serving as deacons, elders, or local pastors. For a full discussion, refer to:

  Part VI: Organization and Administration
  - Chapter Two: The Ministry of the Ordained
  - Section IV. License for Pastoral Ministry (¶¶ 315–320)
  - Section V. Associate Membership (¶¶ 321–323)
  - Section VI. Provisional Membership (¶¶ 324–327)
  - Section VII. The Ordained Deacon in Full Connection (¶¶ 328–330)
  - Section VIII. Appointments of Deacons and Provisional Deacons to Various Ministries (¶ 331)
  - Section IX. The Ordained Elder in Full Connection (¶¶ 332–336); Admission and Continuance of Full Membership in the Annual Conference (¶ 336)
  - Section X. Appointments to Various Ministries (¶¶ 337–342)
  - Section XI. Appointments to Extension Ministries (¶¶ 343–345); Provisions for Appointments to Ecumenical Shared Ministries (¶ 345)

PART II
Yes, No, Maybe

When you begin looking for where God is in your discernment, all your study and prayer about your call and what lies ahead, you may end up exactly where you thought you would, or you may find yourself completely surprised by where God is leading you. Moving from reflecting on your call to acting on it can be joyous and intimidating, exciting and daunting, but what is important is that you continue to be honest with your mentor and group, with God, and with yourself about where you feel God leading you.

Whether you decide at this point to move forward with "yes," "no," or "maybe," keep these in mind:

- God is present and active in your life every day (Joshua 1:9).
- God honors your searching and accompanies you as you search (Proverbs 8:17).
- The Holy Spirit is a strong and sure guide . . . sometimes through a subtle sense of humor, sometimes through the power of a strong wind (Acts 2:1–5).

Moving Forward

Though there are many ways to move toward making a deci-sion, Jesuit Brian McDermott advocates "contemplative" theological reflection for those working toward vocational discernment. Contemplative theological reflection is simple but powerful. For McDermott, contemplative theology builds the kind of relationship with God in which you become close enough to:

- notice what God is like and what God is doing in the world;
- reflect and come to understand more clearly what God is doing;
- become aware of how you are affected by what God is doing; and then
- respond to God and God's call out of this awareness.[27]

As you come to the end of your time with your mentor or candidacy group, the hope is that you have noticed, reflected, and become aware; now is the time to respond.

The chapters in this section are intended to help guide you through the more practical, logistical side of responding. This does not mean discernment stops—we are always dis-cerning our calls. Continue to take your questions to God, to trusted friends, to colleagues. Listen for answers—for yes, for no, for maybe.

Faithfully Following a Call Can Be Disruptive

At the death of her husband, a Maine state trooper, Kate Braestrup was left grief-stricken with four children and the fierce need to find out what she was meant to do with the rest of her life. Like many searchers, she found herself in seminary looking for answers. She found her answer in a most unusual calling: serving as chaplain for search-and-rescue missions in the Maine woods. Reflecting on her seminary training and the training she received working with state and local police, Braestrup came to this realization:

> Law enforcement officers, like all human beings, are presented with grand questions about life's meaning and purpose. They consider the problem of evil, the suffering of innocents, the relationships between justice and mercy, power and responsibility, spirit and flesh. They ponder the impenetrable mystery of death. Cops, in short, think about the same theological issues seminary students research, discuss, argue, and write papers about, but a cop's work lends immediacy and urgency to such questions. Apart from my familiarity with and affinity for police culture, I was sure working with cops would take me right up to where the theological rubber meets the road.[28]

Braestrup's observation fits where you are right now: searching to understand your call, but also moving toward acting on it—where the "rubber meets the road." Open yourself up to hearing compelling calls and uncomfortable ones. This will be invaluable to you as you begin, and continue, making decisions surrounding the candidacy process. It is an adventure, and one that God promises to accompany you on no matter the direction you take.

Chapter Seven
Yes, No, Maybe: Health and Wholeness

It will be a double blessing if you give yourself up to the
Great Physician, that He may heal soul and body together.
And unquestionably this is His design. He wants to give
you . . . both inward and outward health.

—John Wesley[29]

God worked hard for six days and then God rested, per-
forming the consummate act of divine freedom by doing
nothing at all. Furthermore, the rest was so delicious that
God did not call it good, or even very good. Instead, God
blessed the seventh day and called it holy, making Sabbath
the first sacred thing in all creation.

—Barbara Brown Taylor[30]

Holistic Health

United Methodists have a historical foundation of holistic care.
John Wesley was concerned with both the spiritual and physical
health of his clergy and parishioners. In the eighteenth century,

clergy who trained at Oxford or Cambridge attended courses in medical advice as well as theology. Wesley's medical text, *The Primitive Physick*, provided medical advice that was affordable even to the poorest. The most significant aspect of Wesley's book, in addition to the medical advice found in his writings, is his continuous emphasis on preventive care and healthy living.

This makes sense, especially since Jesus's own ministry was holistic: he ministered to many aspects of the people he encountered. The New Testament recounts many times Jesus healed the sick, but he also sent his disciples to pray for them and anoint them.

Our biblical and Wesleyan roots are important. They affirm what we know to be true: health of the clergy directly influences the health of the congregations and communities in which they serve, and vice versa. Your physical, emotional, mental, and spiritual health—including your responses to stress, your understanding of personal values, your ability to set healthy boundaries, and your body's overall health—all of these are part of how the church assesses you as a potential candidate.

Holistic health, the health of the whole person, is crucial to being in ministry as a clergyperson and to live a life of purpose in community and service to others. It is important to note: physical ability is not the bottom line here. *The Book of Discipline* is clear: a disability is not considered an unfavorable health factor (¶ 324.8). What matters is your ability to meet the professional standards and to render effective service in your appointment setting. Whatever your level of ability, the important thing is caring for yourself and honoring the body you have.

This kind of care and attention just might be a little trickier than you think. Many factors affect clergy health:

the 24/7 nature of the position; a lack of adequate support systems; high expectations; and the complex demands of a ministry setting, while also serving the needs of those around you. These factors and more will affect your life if you pursue licensed or ordained ministry.

The sections below discuss different aspects of health, but remember that these aspects are not mutually exclusive. They often overlap and affect one another. As you read this chapter, keep two questions in mind. First, what is the current state of your overall health and your personal behavior in the areas mentioned? Second, what do you need to do to achieve or maintain a healthy balance and healthy behaviors in your life? Greater self-awareness will serve as a great source of strength for your ministry.

Physical Health

You know the litany. Eat fruits and vegetables. Avoid alcohol and other drugs. Exercise. Stay hydrated. Stretch and move around after long sedentary periods. Get enough sleep. Keep a daily balance between work and play. These all may seem like minor adjustments, but they can have major effects on how you function and how you feel.

When the New Testament refers to the body, it often uses the Greek word *soma*. *Soma* encompasses the whole person. In this New Testament way of understanding, it is impossible to separate body from soul. Since your body and your spirit are so intertwined, caring for your body is, in fact, a spiritual discipline.

Unfortunately, some of us are only really attuned to our bodies when we get sick, fatigued, or stressed. In other words, when the balance is off to the point of disrupting our lives. Often, however, it is when we have not been able to take proper care of ourselves that we end up sick, burned-out, or overstressed.

Caring for your body means being connected with it, aware of feelings, sensations, and the messages it constantly sends you. Caring for your body means living *through* your body, not just *in* it.

Consider your daily routine and habits, like how much caffeine you drink throughout the day, the kinds of foods you eat, or how much sleep you get. All of these can affect your health—physical, as well as mental and emotional. How often are you connected with your body? How well do you listen to what it is your body needs? In what ways are you doing well at this, and in what ways might your habits need to change? If you have a chronic illness, what habits and routines center you and help you prepare for the unpredictable?

Remember: your body is not a machine; your body is you, and you are your body. Take that little bit of extra time each day to be aware of your body and its particular needs. Be in tune with the nutrition and food you need as you prepare meals or make food choices. Life can always throw something unexpected our way that can affect our physical health, so it is never a bad time to establish good habits and healthy routines. Every body has limits. Know yours and honor your body in all of its particularity.

Emotional Health

As in everyday life, coping with stress, fostering the ability to understand and manage your feelings, and practicing adaptability in the midst of change are some of the challenges you will face as a minister. One of the best ways to maintain your emotional health is to be aware of your feelings, whether you jump from one emotional extreme to the other, stay steady, or feel little to no emotion. This awareness will go far in helping you handle the stress that inevitably comes and maintain a healthy emotional state.

Nurturing close friendships and a social life will also help you maintain your emotional health. Issues of work/life balance, family pressures, financial stress, anxiety about itineracy and relocation or finding an appointment, relationships with church members and clergy colleagues and supervisors, the spiritual challenges of living authentically—all these will challenge you to maintain a strong emotional awareness so you can address these things from a place of balance. Having friends with whom you can talk openly and confidentially, laugh and express joy, discuss your fears, gain clarity, grieve life's difficulties, and find a listening ear—these will help sustain you and keep you grounded when you need it most.

Maintaining your emotional health is an ongoing process, one that requires attention and care before, during, and after particularly trying seasons. We must take an honest stock of how we might improve. Who makes up your support system? Whom can you ask for help? Are you overcommitted? Are you maintaining physical habits that positively affect your emotional health? Do you have realistic expectations of yourself and of those around you? Have you set proper boundaries? Asking yourself these questions *before* a difficult season arrives will help you weather the storms that come.

Behavioral Health

Behavioral health is another area in which candidates for licensed and ordained ministry are assessed. You have taken (or will take) ministerial and psychological assessments. These assessments provide one source of information as district Committees and Boards of Ordained Ministry select candidates and clergy for licensed and ordained ministry. Psychological assessment provides consultation to applicants and interview committees in the screening and nurture process.

Understanding your behavioral health is important because of the nature of ordained and licensed ministry: a minister works closely with people of all ages, at many different stages of life. The vulnerability of those whom ministers serve must be safeguarded. Trust in clergy is a sacred trust.

Through assessments and interviews, your bearing in the world will be examined and appraised so you may be strengthened to be more durable in the ministry of Christ. Where negatives exist, the examining committee will ask whether these negatives can be sufficiently addressed and understood to enable you to incarnate love in your ministry. Where positives exist, the committee will ask whether these can be used to strengthen trust, enable safety, and express grace, empathy, and love in relationships.

To address these concerns, the Advisory Committee on Candidacy and Clergy Assessment of GBHEM's Division of Ordained Ministry offers a set of *Behavioral Health Guidelines*. These are extensive and will be discussed briefly below. If you wish to read further, the Guidelines are available at http:// www.bomlibrary.org/. Areas of concern in behavioral health include: alcohol and/or drug use and dependency, divorce or infidelity, family violence, general legal issues, sex-related crimes, mental illness, personal finances, physical health, pornography, and sexual misconduct.

The Behavioral Health Guidelines outline standards of behavior that district Committees and Boards of Ordained

Ministry can use when assessing a candidate. Having a mental health need or mental illness does *not* disqualify candidates, but candidates do have to demonstrate their ability to manage their mental health in an ongoing, healthy way.

Take time to look more in-depth at the Behavioral Health Guidelines. If you pursue licensed or ordained ministry, being self-aware will always be critical to your ministry and to the safety of those in your care. Now, as you discern your call, is the time for you to take a careful look at your own behavioral health.

Spiritual Health

In Chapter 4, we walked through some spiritual disciplines that many Christians have practiced and continue to practice. These are important, and you are encouraged to practice a spiritual discipline that daily connects you to God. However, spiritual disciplines are not the whole of our spiritual lives. As much as we must focus on what we *do* to stay spiritually healthy, we must also be attentive to what we *do not do*. As important as it is to ask ourselves, "How often do I pray?" we must also ask, "How often do I rest?"

"God blessed the seventh day and called it holy, making Sabbath the first sacred thing in all creation," Barbara Brown Taylor writes in her book, *An Altar in the World*. Sabbath—or as Taylor puts it, "the practice of saying no"[31] —is a crucial part of our spiritual lives. The demands on the time, schedules, and emotions of those in licensed or ordained ministry can seem limitless. Establishing now the habit of slowing down or stopping completely will help keep you physically, emotionally, mentally, and spiritually well in the days ahead and throughout your life.

You may feel as though taking a full Sabbath day right now is impossible. Perhaps it is. But it is important that, as often as we can, we block off time in our schedules to rest not only when we are sleeping, but also when we are awake. Again, remember that your body is not—that you are not—a machine.

Who are the people in whom you find respite, just by being with them? Where are the physical spaces in which you can find quiet and peace? When was the last time you took a long, deep breath, and then really, *really* exhaled? When was the last time you fully rested in God's presence?

The importance of Sabbath cannot be overstated, as difficult as it may be sometimes to practice it. Sabbath reminds us who God is in the midst of all of our busy-ness—that God is the divine author of our lives, not us, and that life will keep moving even when we take time to stop. "At least one day in every seven," Taylor says,

> Pull off the road and park the car in the garage. Close the door to the toolshed and turn off the computer. Stay home not because you are sick but because you are well. Talk someone you love into being well with you. Take a nap, a walk, an hour for lunch. Test the premise that you are worth more than what you can produce—that even if you spent one whole day being good for nothing you would still be precious in God's sight. . . . Your worth has already been established, even when you are not working.[32]

Test the premise that you are worth more than you can produce. Rest in that truth.

A Life of Health and Balance

Addressing health and wholeness is not a static, once-and-for-all achievement. It is a dynamic experience you live into each day. Decisions you make, hour-by-hour and day-by-day, move you either toward better health and wholeness or away from it. You must make these decisions in the midst of your busy life—within your family and community and in your ministry settings. It is challenging, but the rewards are great. Often, whenever you do take better care of yourself and your body, you are rewarded, sometimes immediately; the body is often adept and responsive to even the smallest steps toward health.

But the responsibility for your health is not yours alone. The ministry settings in which you serve have a responsibility, too. They are, in fact, partners with you in this endeavor. They can help in a variety of ways.

Congregations can help clergy by embracing healthy eating, reducing serving portions, and integrating exercise in their congregational life. Pastor/Staff Parish Relations Committees can provide support for clergy spouses and families by respecting their boundaries and providing them with useful health information and resources. They can also ease the adjustment a clergy family must make when arriving at a new appointment. Clergy can seek support from colleagues and friends as they commit to embrace a healthy work-life balance.

Remember that it is always good to take care of yourself. Take the steps to know what you need to be well. And don't be afraid to invite others into this process to encourage you and help you maintain balance as you pursue God's call in your life.

Reflections

- What does holistic health mean to you? What does the healthiest version of yourself look like? How might that be different from where you are now? Are there areas—nutrition, exercise, sleep, etc.—in which you would like to improve? How might you do that? What strategies or goals might you set for yourself? What are two or three physical practices you would like to improve in the near future?

- What about your emotional health? How would you rate yourself in this category? How do you currently strive to maintain emotional balance? What might be helpful practices for emotional health in the future? And in what ways might your family, friends, and community help you maintain better practices?

- Wesley's book *The Primitive Physick* emphasizes preventive care. What preventive care measures are you practicing? Which would you like to address for yourself? Many health insurance plans cover preventive care. If you have health insurance, are there preventive care benefits you might utilize that currently you are not? Also, find out what clergy health plans, beyond health insurance, are offered by your annual conference—such as gym membership credits, walking challenges, etc.—and how you might benefit from these programs.

- Behavioral health as part of holistic health is critical, yet it is one of the more difficult health measures to talk about and address. Talk with your group about the behavioral health categories mentioned above. How would good health in each of those categories affect ministry? How would dis-ease in each of those categories affect ministry in a congregation?

- Do you practice Sabbath regularly? How often? If you do not practice Sabbath regularly, is there a time in the near future that your schedule might make this more possible? And how might you adjust your schedule now in small ways in order to find moments of rest each day?

- "But the responsibility for your health is not yours alone. The local church (or other setting) in which you serve has a responsibility, too. They are, in fact, partners in this endeavor with you." How do you react to this statement? Is this something you have thought of—or experienced—before? The statement implies that you be able to understand your needs in the many areas of health, and that you find ways to articulate that to others. Can you see yourself being able to do that, or would you have trouble asking for what you need? In what ways can your friends, family, and close community help you identify needs you may be struggling to articulate? How might you be able to encourage conversations and health practice within a ministry setting?

- What is your plan for self-care as you move forward in ministry? Consider all aspects: physical, emotional, behavioral, spiritual, and other types of health. Take time to write out a plan or commitment of ways you will take care of yourself. If you feel comfortable, share your plan with your mentor or mentoring group.

Resources

- *I Believe in the Resurrection of the Body*, by Rubem Alves: This small book, translated from Portuguese, contains a refreshing look at the importance of embodiment. Alves writes that God came to earth as Jesus, because God wanted to live in a human body and experience all the wonderful and mysterious, gratifying and ungratifying, joy-filled and sorrowful things about being a human. (Wipf & Stock Publishing, 2003)
- *Behavioral Health Guidelines*, by the General Board of Higher Education and Ministry of The United Methodist Church: This resource was written to help conference Boards of Ordained Ministry and district Committees on Ordained Ministry address behavioral health as it relates to effectiveness in ministry, as well as the avoidance of misconduct. The Guidelines are intended to assist Boards of Ordained Ministry in the credentialing of candidates for licensed and ordained ministry. Find the Guidelines at http://www.bomlibrary.org/category/health/.
- *Honoring the Body: Meditations on a Christian Practice*, by Stephanie Paulsell: Practical and thoughtful, this book draws on a number of resources from the Christian tradition to help us learn how to celebrate our bodies as they are. Paulsell includes historical resources, Scripture, and stories, and guides readers toward practices that re-shape our understanding of—and our relationship to—our bodies. (Jossey-Bass, 2003)
- *An Altar in the World: A Geography of Faith*, by Barbara Brown Taylor: In this short book, Taylor dedicates each chapter to a different ordinary, daily practice that

awakens our eyes and hearts to God in our lives. "The Practice of Paying Attention," "The Practice of Wearing Skin," and "The Practice of Carrying Water" are just a few of the dozen ordinary tasks Taylor identifies as having the potential to be sacred. Taylor's book encourages readers to pay attention to what is around us, remembering that God is not confined to the four walls of a church building. (HarperOne, 2009)

- *Community and Growth*, by Jean Vanier: As the founder of L'Arche, a network of communities in which disabled adults live with their caretakers, Vanier has gained a lot of wisdom on how to live well in community with others. *Community and Growth* is a reflection on learning who we are in Christ by living in community with others and learning to love others and ourselves as Christ loves us. Though large, this book reads less like a memoir and more like a devotional, offering small pieces of wisdom on which the reader can reflect daily. (Paulist Press, 1989)
- *Primitive Physic: An Easy and Natural Method of Curing Most Diseases*, by John Wesley: First published in the 1740s, the Rev. John Wesley's "Primitive Physick" offered the people of his day both an overall preventive approach to health and a long list of remedies for specific ailments—more than 800 prescriptions for more than 300 different disorders. Though some of his remedies do not translate so well for modern day (for obstructed bowel, "hold a live puppy constantly on the belly"), some of his remedies do hold true even today. (Wipf & Stock, 2003)
- *Living the Sabbath: Discovering the Rhythms of Rest and Delight*, by Norman Wirzba: While Sabbath is often

thought of as just one day a week, Wirzba opens readers up to the notion that Sabbath is much more far-reaching. The rhythms of Sabbath flow through every day, not one. Part of the larger series, "The Christian Practice of Everyday Life," Wirzba's book highlights how those rhythms pulse through our work, our churches, our schools, and other spaces in our daily lives. (Brazos Press, 2006)

- *Center for Health* is an online portal that includes resources, articles, and interactive sites, along with health trends and research, and resources for congregations. Access this website of the General Board of Pension and Health Benefits of The United Methodist Church at www.gbophb.org/center-for-health/.

Chapter Eight
Yes, No, Maybe: Financial Literacy

"If one of you wanted to build a tower, wouldn't you first sit down and calculate the cost, to determine whether you have enough money to complete it? Otherwise, when you have laid the foundation but couldn't finish the tower, all who see it will begin to belittle you. They will say, 'Here's the person who began construction and couldn't complete it!'"

—Luke 14:28–30

. . . know what you own, and why you own it.

—Peter Lynch[33]

Sound financial literacy is a lifelong discipline, but the need to practice diligent financial management is especially important during this time in your life. As you consider your call, it is important to remember that pursuing a life in ministry includes financial implications as well as spiritual ones.

Maybe you are wondering how to pay for graduate school or seminary. Maybe you have already been to graduate school or seminary, but do not know where your call is leading you and what kind of income to expect. Pursuing ministry may not only mean an income change for you, but also for your spouse, or parents, or dependents who rely on you or may have to relocate with you. Whether you have always had a firm grasp on your finances or you have never made a budget, financial literacy will carry you forward and help alleviate, or even prevent, some of the financial burdens of such a major life change.

Goals: Today and Tomorrow

It is difficult to ask for help when we do not know what we need or why we need it. As you meet with your mentor and your candidacy group, begin evaluating both your present and your future goals. Think about your call, your current ministry goals, and also how you hope to clarify those goals or see them change.

Consider also any goals you may have in your personal life. You may be single, married, have children, or have other dependents. You may hope to pursue a specialized area of ministry that requires multiple degrees. All these factors and more affect your finances. Whatever your current or future direction, taking the time now to understand and reflect on what might be required is the first step to managing your finances.

Consider the following as you set your goals:

- **Identify the costs.** It bears repeating: pursuing licensed or ordained ministry includes financial implications as well as spiritual ones. What are the financial costs of pursuing your call (completing education, change of income, itineracy/housing, etc.)? What are the financial risks and benefits? Which costs can you reasonably fund, and with which will you need help? Do you have financial burdens you can reduce, or expunge entirely? Below you will have an opportunity to evaluate your finances in greater detail and further explore the financial implications of pursuing a call to licensed or ordained ministry.

- **Know your timeline.** How long do you have to prepare? Which goals are more pressing, and which can you attend to at a later date? Are you able to prioritize these? Are there certain goals you feel you have little control over? What are the risks involved if you cannot accomplish some of these in time, and what are the financial changes you can anticipate? Consider drawing a timeline or creating a calendar and placing on them important benchmarks, as well as any steps you need to take in order to accomplish them.

- **Ask for help.** Knowing where to find financial support will be crucial as you move forward. If you need to pursue seminary or another graduate degree, first apply for as many scholarships as you can. Ask your school's Financial Aid Office for scholarship suggestions, as they may know about some you do not. Explore United Methodist scholarships offered through the General Board of Higher Education and Ministry, as well as those that may be available through your annual conference, district, or even your local church. If scholarships are not enough, there may still be other options before turning to loans. Many states have public assistance programs available to students who fall below a certain income level. Ask your mentor or candidacy group about financial planning services offered to candidates for assistance. Later in this chapter we will discuss in more detail the best practices in the event that you need to apply for loans.

- **Remember the big picture.** It is easy to be overwhelmed by the finer details. While financial details are important and should be tended diligently, remember to keep the bigger picture in mind. Continuing to discern your call and talking honestly and openly with your mentor and candidacy group about where you feel God leading you will help clarify what's most important.

As you continue this process, remember that as your call changes, so, too, will your goals and your needs. Step back and re-evaluate your finances regularly. Ask yourself what you still need to do, what you have already accomplished, and in what areas you need help. Be honest about your limits. Be gracious to yourself. And remember that God is with you.

Theology and Psychology of Money

Money is a difficult topic. Our experiences with and beliefs about money can evoke a very deep emotional response. Before you evaluate your income and possible expenses, it is important that you are aware of your own theological convictions about money, how money affects you mentally and emotionally, and why. From whom did you learn about money? Perhaps your parents, grandparents, church community, a pastor, or a teacher taught you to see money in a very particular way, or to avoid it completely. How have these experiences shaped you?

We do not make financial decisions in a vacuum. What we believe about money affects how we feel, and vice versa, and influences our decision-making. Below are just a few theological and psychological aspects of money to consider. As you prepare to create your own financial plan, ask how each of these might affect the decisions you make as you discern your call. Write down the ones that weigh heaviest on your heart, and, if you feel comfortable, consider sharing them with your mentor or candidacy group.

- **Tithing.** From Leviticus 27:30–33 and Deuteronomy 26:12–13, to Matthew 5:42 and 2 Corinthians 9:6–7, the Old and New Testaments have a lot to say about regularly giving a portion of your income, how much, and to whom you should give it. While most denominations have a formal or informal system of tithing, some churches put more emphasis on this practice than others. How do you define "tithing"? Do you trust the church to use your tithe money responsibly and honestly? Why or why not? Consider the spiritual discipline of simplicity discussed on page 51. Do your beliefs about tithing extend beyond the offering plate to a life of simplicity, radical giving, or radical hospitality?

- **Fear of scarcity.** There is a big difference between choosing to live with less and being trapped in poverty. For many, an experience of poverty—whether one-time or prolonged—can cause trauma and have a lasting impact on mental, physical, and emotional health. Did you grow up in a household below the poverty line or in an environment riddled with anxiety over finding the next meal or keeping up with bills? Consider how this experience has shaped your identity. How do others react when they learn about your experiences? How might you use your own experiences to minister to others in need? If your financial situation has stabilized, consider how anxiety over money may still persist. What triggers those anxieties, and what calms them?

- **Money as evil.** In Luke's Gospel, Jesus says, "You cannot serve God and wealth" (16:13). And 1 Timothy says, "love of money is the root of all kinds of evil" (6:10). These are difficult passages, especially since money is unavoidable in our daily lives. However, it is important to acknowledge the power dynamic that comes with money and the way that power can be misused. Reflect on how these and other passages, as well as your experience of money misuse, have shaped your perception. What is your understanding of the relationship between wealth and faith? Have you witnessed or experienced manipulation or other misuses of money by others? How has that experience formed you? Consider also your church and community, how they reflect or differ from your own convictions. How might you practice ministry differently in a ministry setting with members who are predominantly wealthier or poorer than you?

- **Blessing and prosperity.** Stories of material blessing as a reward for faithfulness seem to saturate the Old Testament, like the blessing of Sarah and Abraham in Genesis 17 with descendants and land, for example, or the blessing of Solomon in 2 Chronicles 1 with wealth, honor, and possessions. While some churches fully subscribe to prosperity theology—the belief that faith and positivity (among other things) will increase believers' material wealth—many non-prosperity churches teach

112

a watered-down version of this theology, often unknowingly. What have you been taught about material blessing and God's favor? How have you learned about struggle, loss, or tragedy—and God's role in times of turmoil? Do you believe, or has someone in your life told you, that the financial implications of pursuing ministry are signs of God's approval or disapproval? How has this affected you as you discern God's call in your life?

- **Means to an end.** Learning how to manage money properly can be difficult, especially if you were taught that money is merely a means to an end, and never taught proper boundaries or limits. For some, this may manifest in irresponsible spending or the inability to prioritize bills over entertainment. For others, the inability to set boundaries with money may reveal a deeper problem, such as an addiction or an unhealthy consumption practice. Lack of accountability around budgeting and spending can lead to disastrous financial problems. What is your understanding of the balance between paying bills and paying for luxuries? What helps you decide whether or not to "splurge" on a luxury? Keep a record of the money you spend over the next week. Examine how your spending might reveal an unhealthy balance in how you use your money. Consider, then, how your personal spending habits will influence your skills and decisions in managing a church or business budget.

- **Clergy as financial leaders.** Wherever you may end up serving, you will be seen as someone who should be supportive of the full ministry of your appointment setting. This includes supporting the Church's work financially. As you consider being an example for others who are making decisions about tithing and church-based giving, what thoughts or concerns do you have about being an example to others? What potential for ministry do you see in relationship to your own giving to the Church?

These are just a few aspects to consider as you move forward. If there are other theological or psychological aspects to money that have been particularly formative for you, write them down or consider sharing those as well. For many of us, money is a difficult topic to discuss, often because we have experiences with it that made us feel ashamed, afraid, or hurt. It is important to be aware of what we believe and how we feel about money so we can acknowledge where we might need healing or growth.

A Closer Look

Now that you have identified your goals and reflected on your beliefs and experiences, it is time to crunch the numbers. There are many aspects to consider when building a healthy financial plan. How much are you spending? How much are you saving? Will you need to borrow money to make ends meet? Is investment an option? Can you provide for unexpected future risks or emergencies? All of these are integral to sound financial management.

At the end of this chapter is a "Planning for Ministry Financial Worksheet." Complete this worksheet. This exercise may take a while and may require you to gather certain financial information or documents. If you do not have access to exact numbers for certain lines, estimate as best as you can.

The following sections will help you identify and remember important pieces of your financial picture.

Income and Funding

The basic tool for building a financial plan is having an accurate picture of your total income and how it might change. Income includes scholarships, grants, investments, savings, and contributions from family (spouse, parents, etc.) or friends, as well as employment. Be sure to also include irregular or inconsistent income.

Now consider how any or all of these will change by attending graduate school or seminary, or entering ministry, and what new or unexpected costs may arise. Will you still be able to work while attending school? Does going back to school mean a switch from full-time to part-time employment? If you need to relocate, how might that affect your spouse's income, as well as your own? Is the minimum or average salary of a deacon, elder, or local pastor in a similar ministry setting comparable to your current income, or would you be taking a pay cut? How will your ability to save, health benefits, or retirement contributions change? Take into account all aspects of your current and (projected) future income.

Spending

Now that you have calculated your income, evaluate your spending. How much do you spend every month on housing (including utilities, homeowners or renters insurance, taxes)? What about insurance (medical, car, etc.)? A cell phone? Educational loan, personal loan, or credit card payments? Do you bike, walk, take public transportation, drive a car? Do you regularly tithe or donate to charity? Are you currently funding your own education—tuition, books, fees—for a different degree? What about incidental expenses, such as car repairs, home maintenance, unforeseen medical bills, or clothing? Remember to include unexpected or irregular costs like entertainment, travel, or other luxuries or non-essential items. Read over your last few bank statements to make sure you aren't forgetting any bills.

Just as you did with your income, write down your expenses. Consider how any or all of these may change by going to seminary, or entering part- or full-time ministry. Will you need to fund part or all of your tuition, books, and fees for graduate school, seminary, or licensing school? Will you drive more often or farther distances? If you need to move for school or a new ministry setting, is the cost of living higher or lower in that new location? Will your mode of transportation change? How might moving, going back to school, or entering ministry affect your spouse's expenses or certain costs for your dependent(s)? Evaluate all aspects of your current and (projected) future spending.

Long-Term Borrowing

For many, educational loans are an unavoidable reality. The cost of higher education continues to rise, along with student debt levels, which means many future clergy will need to plan for loan repayment. While living within your means and reducing costs now can help reduce how much you borrow, it is still important to know your numbers and plan accordingly.

- **Know your numbers.** According to http://finaid.org, each $10,000 of student loan debt repaid over a ten-year period with a 6.8 percent interest rate requires a monthly payment of $115.08. If you take out a total of $60,000, your payments will be $690 a month over a ten-year period.[34] Before you borrow any money, know exactly how much the interest rate is and what the monthly repayment amount would be. You can also use the Loan Calculator on http://finaid.org or websites like http://unbury.me to find out exactly how long it would take you to repay your loans with various monthly payments. Include payments for any undergraduate education or any outstanding credit card loans you may have. Remember: even though payments on some loans may not be required while you are in school, the interest on these loans may continue to build, which can increase the principal amount owed.[35] Consider reducing overall total payments toward these loans by making payments while in school. Take advantage of lowering interest rates some borrowers offer by signing up for automated draft payments. Also, while you are still in school, many banks offer automated interest rate reductions for Automated Clearing House (ACH) payments.

- **Know your options.** As mentioned above, explore scholarships and other forms of assistance before considering student loans. If loans are necessary, research and shop for lenders with the lowest interest rates. Meet with your school's financial aid office and ask how you might take out the minimum amount in loans with the lowest percentage rates possible in order to cover your education only. Then find other means to cover your living expenses. Ask if you can borrow on a month-to-month basis, rather than taking out a flat amount at the beginning of each semester. There are also programs for those who work in public service or nonprofit organizations that allow for some percentage of federal student loans to be forgiven after a certain number of years; however, there are limitations as to what professions and loans qualify. There are also programs that limit the monthly repayment amount based on salary. Again, knowing what your payments would be, how long they would last, and which loans qualify for forgiveness *before* you borrow is essential. Many seminaries offer educational programs to teach students financial literacy and increase their understanding of budgeting and debt. Discuss your options and receive guidance for building your financial plan from the school(s) you hope to attend.

- **Know your income.** Do your expected monthly student loan payments equal 10 percent or less of your expected monthly net income? If yes, reconsider whether taking out loans is the only option or if another expense might be sacrificed instead. Or if you cannot sacrifice an expense now, are there costs you may be able to reduce or even eliminate in the future? Knowing if your student debt will be manageable can help maintain your future financial health. Careful, diligent, and regular re-evaluation of your current and future financial situation can help you avoid borrowing more than absolutely necessary.

The Expense of Expenses

John Wesley said, "We ought to gain all we can gain . . . but this it is certain we ought not to do; we ought not to gain money at the expense of life, nor at the expense of our health."[36] Money can be a source of immense stress in our lives. There will always be expenses we cannot foresee. Our lives will go in directions we did not anticipate.

Be aware of your limits—physically, mentally, emotionally, and financially. Evaluate your finances regularly and continue looking for different options. That way, when the unpredictable happens, you are prepared. Do not let stress or worry about financial management come at the expense of life or the expense of your health. Faithfully discerning and pursuing God's call for your life is always the goal.

Reflections

- How has your upbringing affected the way you feel about or use money? Do you follow the practices your parents, grandparents, or other elders instilled in you, or do you actively approach money differently than you were taught?
- What most applied to you in the "Theology and Psychology of Money" section? Did it reveal anything new about the way you approach or avoid money? Is there an area in particular in which you need further growth, healing, or accountability, and how might you pursue that?
- Look at your completed Financial Planning for Ministry Worksheet. What expenses surprised you? What patterns or inconsistencies did you notice? What will be the biggest financial challenge for you as you move forward?

- What funding resources mentioned in this chapter are worth pursuing? Are there other options for funding or support that were not mentioned in this chapter?
- Talk with your mentor or candidacy group about programs or resources offered by your annual conference to assist candidates and clergy in gaining a better understanding of how to manage personal and church finances. Is there an area of personal or church financial management you find particularly challenging?

Resources

- *Being Consumed: Economics and Christian Desire*, by William T. Cavanaugh: Globalization, consumption, economics—are these topics about which Christians should have an opinion? How much do we reflect on our personal and communal practices of consumption, and what difference does it make? With sacramental theology and a deeper understanding of the Eucharist at its core, Cavanaugh's book pushes Christians to take a harder look at what they consume—and at what consumes them. This is a good resource for anyone interested in theologically-based alternative economic practices. (Wm. B. Eerdmans Publishing Co., 2008)
- *Money Rules: The Simple Path to Lifelong Security*, by Jean Chatzky: In a time of financial uncertainty or change, this book by *Today* show's financial expert is a great resource. The bottom line, she says: money is simple—people make it complicated. Chatzky gives some basic yet crucial approaches to spending, saving, investing,

and finding financial balance. Her extra Dos and Don'ts section is especially helpful. (Rodale Books, 2012)

- *Happy Money: The Science of Spending Happier*, by Elizabeth Dunn and Michael Norton: This tour of research on the science of spending explains how you can get more happiness for your money. Dunn and Norton outline five principles—from choosing experiences over stuff to spending money on others— to guide not only individuals looking for financial security, but also companies seeking to create happier employees and provide "happier products" to their customers. Their five core principles of smart spending are both pragmatic and visionary. (Simon and Schuster, 2014)

- *Your Faith, Your Finance: A Guide to Money, Faith and Ethics*, by The Ecumenical Council for Corporate Responsibility (ECCR) and Quaker Peace & Social Witness (QPSW): This website raises questions and provides resources for reflection on money and its place in Christians' lives. From the theological (money in the Bible) to the pragmatic (how you can be an ethical spender), this resource provides engaging material for thought, along with helpful study guides for individuals and for churches. http://www.yourfaithyourfinance.org/.

- *Money and Ministry: A Practical Guide for Pastors*, by Janet T. Jamieson and Philip D. Jamieson: This poignant and practical resource will help you develop a sound theology of money, and then put that theology of money to work in your everyday life in ministry. Topics range from a history of the Church's teachings on money, to church finances and budgeting, to money in your personal life and beyond. (Westminster John Knox Press, 2009)

- *Office of Loans and Scholarships,* the General Board of Higher Education and Ministry: The United Methodist Scholarship and Loan Program is a church-wide educational service providing scholarships and loans to help supplement students' financial needs. Funding is provided through offerings, wills, annuities, and other designated gifts. Visit http://www.gbhem.org/loansandscholarships.

- *Making the Most of Your Money Now,* by Jane Bryant Quinn: This comprehensive guidebook steers you around the risks and helps you make smart and profitable decisions at every stage of your life—single, married, divorced, first job, later in your career. Subjects include: setting priorities during and after a financial setback, credit and debit card practices that will save money, the simplest ways to pull yourself out of debt, why it's so important to participate in an automatic savings plan, and ideas for keeping your credit scores in shape. (Simon and Schuster, 2010)

- *Total Money Makeover: A Proven Plan for Financial Fitness,* by Dave Ramsey: Radio and television show host and financial expert, Ramsey addresses myths about debt and money, shows how to design a plan for paying off all debt, gives practical ways for saving and securing a strong financial future, and provides a road map for making over money habits. This is one of his most accessible books. (Thomas Nelson, 2010)

- *Personal Finance for Dummies,* by Eric Tyson: This combines Tyson's time-tested financial advice along with updates to his strategies that reflect changing economic conditions. He includes techniques for tracking expenditures, reducing spending, and getting out from under the burden of high-interest debt. Updated for today's economy, this guide provides concrete advice for anyone facing financial hardship and recommends where to go for more help. (For Dummies, 2012)

- *Personal Finance in Your 20s for Dummies,* by Eric Tyson: Another in the Dummies series, this book provides sound, reliable advice on how to make smart financial choices in the real world. Geared toward college students, recent graduates, and those planning to continue their education. (John Wiley & Sons, 2011)

Planning for Ministry Financial Worksheet
Estimated Income & Financial Assistance

INCOME	MONTHLY	ANNUAL
Child Support Payments Received	$_____	$_____
Guaranteed Income (Social Security, VA, etc.)	$_____	$_____
Spouse Earnings	$_____	$_____
Student Earnings	$_____	$_____
Other (specify): _____	$_____	$_____
Other (specify): _____	$_____	$_____
Total Income	$_____	$_____

Financial Assistance

	MONTHLY	ANNUAL
Annual Conference Scholarships/Support	$_____	$_____
Educational Scholarships (University/Seminary)	$_____	$_____
Family/Friends	$_____	$_____
Grants	$_____	$_____
GBHEM Scholarships	$_____	$_____
Home Church/Congregational Support	$_____	$_____
Ministerial Education Fund (MEF) Support	$_____	$_____
Other (specify): _____	$_____	$_____
Other (specify): _____	$_____	$_____
Total Financial Assistance	$_____	$_____

Current Assets

Automobiles
(value less any amount owed) $_____ $_____
Cash and Savings $_____ $_____
Investments (CDs, stocks, etc.) $_____ $_____
Properties/Real Estate $_____ $_____
Retirement Savings
(IRAs, 401Ks, etc.) $_____ $_____
Other (specify): _____ $_____ $_____
Other (specify): _____ $_____ $_____
Total Current Assets $_____ $_____

**Total Estimated
Financial Resources** $_____ $_____

ESTIMATED EXPENSES   MONTHLY ANNUAL

Educational Expenses

Annual Tuition $_____ $_____
Books $_____ $_____
Candidacy/Ordination Process Fees $_____ $_____
Educational Fees $_____ $_____
Special Programs
(CPE, Internship, etc.) $_____ $_____
Other (specify): _____ $_____ $_____
Other (specify): _____ $_____ $_____
Total Educational Expenses $_____ $_____

Living Expenses

Automobile Payments	$_____	$_____
Automobile Insurance	$_____	$_____
Child Care	$_____	$_____
Child Support Payments	$_____	$_____
Clothing	$_____	$_____
Dependent Allowance	$_____	$_____
Food and Household Supplies	$_____	$_____
Health Insurance	$_____	$_____
Incidentals	$_____	$_____
Life Insurance Premiums	$_____	$_____
Other Medical/Dental	$_____	$_____
Prescriptions	$_____	$_____
Rent/Mortgage Payment	$_____	$_____
Telecommunications (Phone, Cell, Internet, etc.)	$_____	$_____
Tithe and Other Charitable Donations	$_____	$_____
Transportation	$_____	$_____
Utilities	$_____	$_____
Other (specify): _____	$_____	$_____
Other (specify): _____	$_____	$_____
Total Living Expenses	$_____	$_____
Combined Total Estimated Expenses	$_____	$_____
Total Income Less Expenses	$_____	$_____

INDEBTEDNESS

Indebtedness*

Indebtedness*	Candidate	Spouse
Educational Loans: Undergrad & Grad		
Principal Balance: Monthly Pmt.	$_____	$_____
Principal: Monthly Pmt.	$_____	$_____
Federal Perkins Loans	$_____	$_____
Fed. Subsidized Stafford	$_____	$_____
Fed. Unsubsidized Stafford	$_____	$_____
GBHEM/UMC Loans	$_____	$_____
Loans from Parents/Family	$_____	$_____
Other Educational Loans	$_____	$_____
Estimated Future Loans	$_____	$_____
Totals	$_____	$_____

Non-Educational Debt

	Candidate	Spouse
Mortgage	$_____	$_____
Credit Cards	$_____	$_____
Other (specify): _____	$_____	$_____
Other (specify): _____	$_____	$_____
Other (specify): _____	$_____	$_____
Other (specify): _____	$_____	$_____
Other (specify): _____	$_____	$_____
Totals	$_____	$_____

Combined Indebtedness Totals $_____ $_____

*Candidate's (and spouse's) current indebtedness.
Report principal amounts and related monthly payments.
† These pages are reproducible.

Chapter Nine
Yes, No, Maybe: Next Steps

"I think it would be well, and proper, and obedient, and pure, to grasp your one necessity and not let it go, to dangle from it limp wherever it takes you.

—Annie Dillard[37]

I love Jesus for the shaft of light that he throws across the pathway of those who seek to answer the question, What shall I do with my life?

—Howard Thurman[38]

With the hope that this candidacy process has shed some light across your path, it is time for next steps. Deacon, elder, local pastor, ministry as a layperson: different options, different calls, different answers. Your call may look similar to that of others in your candidacy group. Your answer—yes, no, or maybe—may be similar as well. Or the call and the answer may be very different. Whichever the case, your next steps will be as unique to you as God's relationship with you. As you discuss your decisions with your candidacy group, remember this: your call may look different from everyone else's; it is still a valid call.

Gaining Clarity

Consider these questions below to help you gather your thoughts and insights once more as you decide what is next. You may want to write your responses, journal your impressions, or discuss them with your mentor or group.

- How does your call show itself right now—as feelings, images, in the voices of those around you?
- Recall the people or instances that have helped you better understand your call. Whose influence seems to move you toward a "yes" answer? Whose guidance might be steering you more toward saying "no" at this time? Whose feedback could lead you to a "maybe" decision?
- Your ego (self-esteem, sense of self-worth, notion of self-identity) can be a skillful asset or a powerful liability in discerning your call. Examine the place of your ego in this process. How can you know whether your ego is providing more truth than fiction about your call? How might your ego muffle or distort your call?
- What conversations do you need to have right now to provoke you toward a clearer answer of "yes," "no," or "maybe"? Are there voices you have not yet heard or need to hear in a different way? Is there some part of your inner voice that needs to speak more deeply to you as you move toward a decision?

Three Possibilities Ahead

Yes. No. Maybe. Three possible answers to the question you seek to answer: "What shall I do with my life?" Will you pursue ordination as a deacon or an elder? Will you seek licensing as a local pastor? Will you embrace and expand your ministry as a layperson? Do you need more time and more clarity?

As a start toward your next steps, try to summarize your call and your response to that call in one or two sentences: "I feel called to [type of ministry] because [reasons]. Write this down on an index card or sheet of paper. Take it with you to your mentor group meeting. Ask this question of members of your group: "What form of ministry, in your opinion, suits my gifts best?" Note their responses on the back of your card or paper. Take in as much information as you can. Does anyone's response surprise you? Reinforce your understanding of yourself? Challenge you?

As you and others do this same reflection for each group member, stay alert for new information or insights. Keep in mind again that while there may be similarities between your call and others' calls, your call might look very different from anyone else's. God's relationship with each person is different.

Answering "No"

By being faithful to your discernment around licensed or ordained ministry, you may decide your Christian work is in the ministry of the laity. If "no" is your decision, your mentor, your candidacy group, and your church will support you.

You can relate what you have learned and the insights you have gained to exploring other careers as your response to God's grace and love for you. You may want to discuss other career issues with your mentor, and later let your mentor know of your next plans and decisions. The United Methodist Church supports a number of possible avenues for lay ministry, including Lay Servant Ministries and Certified Lay Ministry. Your mentor or district Committee may be able to help you in seeking one of these avenues for possible ministry as well.

You can also return at a later time to this step in the candidacy process to look further into licensed or ordained ministry. "No" today is not a once-and-forever decision. It is an important decision, but it is not *the* most important decision you make. Your decision to serve God *each day* is the most notable mark of your calling—no matter the setting.

Answering "Maybe"

You may still be undecided about whether to become a candidate for licensed or ordained ministry. In any career decision, there is uncertainty. Ask your mentor, your group, or other people if they have experienced this in their own life decisions. Uncertainty is part of life; no one can predict the future. As Christians, we know God holds the future and will accompany us into it.

Talk with your mentor about your uncertainties, both in vocation and in your wider life. Discuss where you are now in your decision and whether your "maybe" is a good decision for you at this time in your life. You might ask for continuing discussions with your mentor or with others as you continue to clarify your call to a career. There may be ways your mentor can help guide you to a decision point.

Answering "Yes"

Through self-awareness and attentiveness, your work in discernment may bring you to answer "yes" to the call to licensed or ordained ministry. This decision reflects your best understanding of where God is calling you now. It is a major decision; it is important that you continue to pay attention to God's leading. As you move forward, God's call for you will grow and change. Even if you say yes today, be prepared to hear more as God's call evolves—sometimes in ways that confirm your decision today, and sometimes in ways that could challenge it.

Honoring Our Passages

As you prepare to move on, take time to honor and pay tribute to the calls you and your group have explored, the decisions you each have made, and the gifts of grace and insight that have come through this time with your mentor and your group. Listen carefully as each group member talks about her or his decision. Spend time in prayer for each person, asking for God's continued blessings and guidance for each of them.

Together with your group, come up with a short ritual or liturgy of sending forth. Find a way to bless, as a worshipping community, the next steps each of you will undertake in the coming weeks and months. Honor the covenant you made with your group at the beginning of this process with a leave-taking pledge of continued support.

If you have come to a "yes" decision about going forward to request becoming a certified candidate for licensed or ordained ministry, you need to know what is next with your local church's Pastor/Staff Parish Relations Committee, its charge conference, and the district Committee on Ordained Ministry. Check with your mentor or annual conference representative about the specific process requirements for your conference. Remember that your decision to pursue candidacy means you are offering yourself to the church, which will then make the decision about whether or not to confirm you as a candidate for licensed or ordained ministry. Below is an outline of what happens next.

Recommendation by Your Local Ministry Setting

It is now time for you to share what you have learned about yourself, God's grace, your gifts for ministry, and your calling with your pastor and with your local church's Pastor/Staff Parish Relations Committee (or its equivalent, if you are coming from a collegiate ministry or other setting).

- **Meeting with your pastor.** Most likely you have already talked with your pastor, collegiate minister, or another clergyperson about your candidacy studies. If you have, this meeting will further the conversation and bring your pastor up to date. If you have not, this meeting will give you a chance to describe your experiences and your decision to apply for candidacy. You will also give or send your pastor a letter asking for a recommendation from your church's charge conference.
- **Meeting with the Pastor/Staff Parish Relations or Local Committee.** Your pastor will help arrange a meeting with your local church's (or other ministry's) Pastor/Staff Parish Relations Committee. This committee has responsibility on behalf of both the local church and the larger United Methodist Church

whether to recommend you to the district Committee as a candidate. There is no prescribed format for this meeting, other than that together you discuss Wesley's historic questions about grace, gifts, and fruits for ministry as found in *The Book of Discipline* (¶ 310). You should provide a statement of your call and be prepared to discuss your discernment process. Committee members may ask questions about your life experience, your decision, your hopes and expectations, as well as your promise for effectiveness in licensed or ordained ministry. The committee is encouraged not to give a yes vote lightly. If your calling and decision are to be supported by the Church, both can stand the test of careful inquiry and examination.

- **Meeting with your charge conference (or its equivalent).** If your Pastor/Staff Parish Relations Committee approves you, you will come before the local church's charge conference (or the designated group in another ministry setting) for a recommendation. If this group approves you, you will be referred to the district Committee on Ordained Ministry. Be prepared to discuss in depth about your call and to answer any questions the charge conference might have.

District Committee on Ordained Ministry

The district Committee's priority is to find the best possible leadership for licensed and ordained ministry. Their responsibility is to supervise all matters surrounding candidacy for licensed or ordained ministry.

- Preparation for the meeting. You will provide a series of reflections and documents as background for this meeting, including:

  > Your written statement of call
  > Your mentor's report
  > A psychological assessment
  > Background reports and credit checks
  > Additional information required by ¶ 310 of *The Book of Discipline* (2012)
  > Any other information required by your annual conference

- **Meeting.** In your meeting with the district Committee, the intention is for every person to be as open and candid about you and the candidacy process as possible. You will have time to express your understanding of who you are and how God is calling you. If your mentor attends the district Committee meeting with you, she/he may be asked to share their report. (Mentors function only as observers, with their sole input being their report.) Committee members will have questions for you. These may include wanting to know more about your call, family or financial questions, or your plans for continuing your education. If you are unclear about anything in the conversation, ask for clarification. An open, back-and-forth discussion is the best way for the committee to get to know you.
- **Deliberation.** After the discussion, committee members will deliberate together on your candidacy; they will consider your statement of call, your answers to

their questions, and all documents and reports they have received. (As a matter of annual conference policy, the district Committee will decide whether or not you will be present during their deliberation.) After their consideration, members of the committee will vote on your certification by written ballot. A three-fourths majority is needed for approval for certification.

District Committee Decision

In addition to their vote, the district Committee will offer suggestions and counsel, as well as give you a clear explanation of the reasons for their decision. They may make one of three decisions:

- **Yes.** If they decide to certify you as a candidate for licensed or ordained ministry, the district Committee will inform you. They may offer insights and suggestions based on the members' contacts with you. In addition, your candidacy mentor, district superintendent, pastor, and many others are available to you as consultants in your decisions about education and continuing preparation for licensed or ordained ministry.
- **Deferred or Delayed.** If district Committee members have substantial uncertainties about your candidacy, it is important for them to delay a decision until their questions are clarified. The committee may inform you that further information or other work will be necessary before a decision is made. It is the responsibility of the committee to be clear and open with you and your mentor about the nature of their uncertainties and to offer appropriate counsel to you.

- **No.** If they decide not to certify you as a candidate, they will give you reasons for this decision directly, either during or immediately following the meeting. They may also make suggestions to you about any options or decisions you may have from there. Your candidacy mentor is also available to help interpret opinions and alternatives for both you and the committee.

Regardless of the district Committee's decision, it is their responsibility to provide—and the candidate's right to receive—written notification for all decisions related to candidacy, licensing, and ordination.

Reporting the Decision

A representative from your conference will record the district Committee's decision about your candidacy—yes, deferred/delayed, no—along with any of their recommendations. While the committee—in cooperation with the Board of Ordained Ministry—determines the details of the reporting process, in most cases a record of the outcome is the only report needed.

The decision will be recorded at the appropriate place at the online enrollment site (umcares.org) where you have enrolled as a candidate.

Pentimento: The Painting Changes

Pentimento. It is a word borrowed from Italian often used in the art world. It denotes an alteration in a painting, evidenced by traces of the artist's previous work, presented in a new, changed composition. Earlier images, forms, or strokes have been changed and painted over. The artist's earlier ideas have been painted over, changed—but the original work remains as a base.

Pentimento. It is a process not unlike the one you are in now. Earlier decisions are formed and then re-formed as you listen for God's call. Your call and your formation are never finished. You—and all of us—are always beginning again, renewing, and sometimes reforming who we are as a called people. Through all these passages, at each and every turn, God meets us, journeys with us, protects us, and encourages us.

Trust in God. Trust yourself. Trust the path ahead of you, even when you are not quite sure where it leads.

Reflections

- Talk about your current understanding of your call with your mentor and group. Listen to others in the group talk about their calls. How is your call similar? How is it different?
- Name times you have seen Jesus's "shaft of light" across your path as you have discerned what to do with your life. Have these shafts of light been people, readings, events that happened in the world? What difference have these moments made for you?
- Spend some time answering the questions under "Gaining Clarity." As you explore these questions, make notes of what emerges for you. Share these with your mentor and with your group.
- In this chapter you were invited to reflect on your call and your response to it. Share your reflections with your mentor or mentor group. Ask, "What form of ministry, in your opinion, suits my gifts best?" Does

anyone's response reinforce or challenge your understanding of yourself?

- Your answer to whether you are being called to ordained or licensed ministry might be "no." If so, discuss with your mentor and group what your next steps will be in discerning your call. If your answer is "maybe," discuss what your next steps might be. If your answer is "yes," look at the next steps outlined in this chapter, which you will take with your local church or collegiate ministry to apply for the candidacy process; make sure your mentor or another annual conference representative provides you with clear steps to follow through the candidacy, licensing, and ordination process.

Resources

- *The Book of Discipline of The United Methodist Church (2012)*, Section III. Candidacy for Licensed and Ordained Ministry (¶¶ 310–314): These paragraphs of *The Book of Discipline* lay out the particular requirements of candidacy for licensing and ordination in The United Methodist Church. It is important for you to read these paragraphs and become familiar with their contents, as they will be an invaluable resource to you along the journey toward licensing or ordination. Additionally, you will need to check with your annual conference about the specific process for candidacy certification in your area.
- There is a lot to remember as you go through the candidacy process. Be sure to bookmark the "Starting Candidacy" web page, which has lots of tips and tricks

to help you as you begin. See http://umcandidacy.org to find the information you need as you go along.

- If you feel called to pursue licensing, you will need to complete Licensing School and the Basic Course of Study, which is prescribed by the General Board of Higher Education and Ministry of The United Methodist Church (¶ 1421.3d). To learn more about licensing school, curricula, and Advanced Course of Study, visit http://www.gbhem.org/education/licensing-and-course-study.

- If you feel called to pursue ordination and seminary as part of your next steps, you will need to attend a United Methodist seminary or a non-United Methodist seminary approved by the University Senate (¶ 324.4). To learn about the 13 United Methodist seminaries or find out what other seminaries the University Senate has approved, visit http://www.gbhem.org/education/seminary.

Appendix A
Mentor Guide

Part I / Chapter 1
Mentoring and Candidacy Groups

This section outlines important background, processes, and values for mentors, candidates, and the candidacy group. Prepare for this group meeting by reading the Introduction and the Mentoring and Candidacy Groups chapters. Also, prepare an opening meditation or devotion for the group. You may ask candidates to lead this in future meetings.

In this first meeting, candidates will start getting acquainted with each other. They will begin learning each other's stories. Prepare the environment to help them become comfortable and feel safe sharing in the group.

The Introduction brings up the broad subject of call, noting that calls can be subtle or obvious, gentle or unsettling. Ask the group to discuss this, especially as it relates to where they are right now in the discernment process. Share your own experiences and story as well.

Below are some of the major points in these first sections. Guide your group in discussion and interaction around these issues:

- Discuss the relationship between mentor and candidate, candidate and group, and mentor and the group: what a mentor is (and is not), what it means to be exploring candidacy for ministry, how the companionship of a group can be helpful in personal discernment.
- Consider the mutual commitment of participating in a group: including the place of confidentiality, regular participation, hospitality, and openness to everyone in your group.
- Discuss the significance and place of prayer in the group's life, the pivotal role of spiritual support among group members, and the impact of strong spiritual disciplines in the life of the group.

Covenant

This section suggests the group develop a covenant and includes some guidelines for how to do this. Discuss the components of the covenant—presence, prayer, hospitality, and confidentiality. Invite group members to make changes or additions to this covenant, or to write one of their own. You may want to present some Scripture to guide a conversation about covenants (e.g., Jeremiah 31:31–34). When the covenant is firm, each group member should sign it, along with you as mentor. Make sure everyone in the group gets a signed copy of the covenant and encourage them to reflect on it often; perhaps include a reminder at the beginning of each meeting.

Framework and Outline for Meetings

Your annual conference will most likely set the overall structure of your candidacy group. Go over with your group matters such as dates and timelines, number of meetings, and framework and content of those meetings, along with any additional requirements and deadlines. Be clear about your expectations for the meetings and whether your conference allows online/video participation. Be sure to check the resources in the back of this book to see examples from some annual conferences, which may be helpful to you.

The Candidacy Process in Your Annual Conference

It is essential that candidates understand how the candidacy process works in your conference. Stages, dates, forms, and deadlines should be part of this. Share with the group your conference's step-by-step guide to this process. Begin with a person's first contact for entry into the candidacy process and continue through the interview with the district Committee on Ordained Ministry.

Prepare a written "road map" of this process, or use the guide produced by your conference. Highlight with your group the major steps along the way, noting important dates and deadlines. Answer questions. Let the group know you are available to them as they go through this process.

Discuss the function of the report that you, as mentor, will make for each group member at the end of this process. Let them know this report goes to the district Committee on Ordained Ministry as a partial introduction of them to the committee. Share with them some of the facets of this one-page report: the candidate's self-awareness, gifts for ministry, articulation of call, and your observation of their faith journey thus far.

Emphasize that because of the mutual confidentiality covenant you share with candidates, the candidate must approve in writing anything you share in this report. Candidates will have the chance to read, sign, and talk with you about the report before you, as their mentor, send it to the district Committee. Answer any questions they may have about the mentor's report.

(In a later chapter you will find more specific suggestions for preparing this report.)

Closing

Plan a closing time with your group. You could ask for brief reactions or reflections on the group's session together. Prepare the group for the next meeting by discussing any reading or other tasks they need to complete before that meeting.

In addition, part of this time might be used to check in with individuals on their place or progress in the conference's process toward a possible certification interview with the district Committee, and to see if they have any questions about this. You may feel it is too early to do this, or you may prefer to check in one-on-one. Use your judgment as to the best way to keep track of your group members' progress. Continue to let them know you are available to help them along the way.

Design a closing ritual or time of prayer. You may decide to close with the same ritual every session or to close in different ways each time. Most likely you will be the one to lead the closing of this first session; going forward, you may want to ask different group members to lead.

Part I / Chapter 2
Our Theological Task, General Rules, Connectional-ism, Mission, and the Social Principles

This section outlines major United Methodist theological and connectional principles. Prepare for this group meeting by reading Chapter 2, "What United Methodists Believe: Our Theological Task, General Rules, Connectionalism, Mission, and the Social Principles," as well as their corresponding paragraphs in *The Book of Discipline*. Prepare an opening meditation or devotion for the group, or introduce the group member who will do this.

Candidates will continue getting acquainted with each other. Prepare the environment to help them become comfortable and feel safe sharing in the group. You might begin the meeting by asking one or two short questions inviting group members to tell a little more about themselves, such as "Which Bible passage sustains you or gives you joy when you read it?" or "What was the best (or worst) thing that happened to you since we last met?" You may also want to ask some quick preliminary questions of the group about the reading material in this section, such as "What most surprised you about this chapter?" or "What did you find most interesting or compelling about this reading?"

Invite the group to discuss some of the reflection questions at the end of the chapter. Ask candidates to focus on the intersection between their beliefs and those of United Methodism, as outlined in the reading.

The Theological Task of United Methodist Laity and Clergy

Enable discussion and reflection that helps clarify the theological task of United Methodists. Highlight the four central principles of our theological reflections: (1) critical and constructive, (2) individual and communal, (3) contextual and incarnational, and (4) essentially practical. Explore these principles by asking the group for concrete examples of each principle. Be prepared to contrast these theological principles with those of other denominations or religious traditions.

General Rules and Small Groups

Wesley's understanding of grace, the General Rules, and small groups is critical to understanding United Methodism. Have the group "translate" Wesley's General Rules into contemporary language. What impact might accountability to a small group and to these Rules have on their lives?

Connectionalism and Mission

Our denomination's connectional ties are one of The United Methodist Church's greatest strengths. This meeting offers an opportunity for your group to survey the impact of our connectionalism. Using the three categories of faith and good works, mission and service, and connectionalism for mission, review how our accountability to and connection with others enriches both our common life and our mission in the world. Contrast that with the structure of other denominations that are congregationally-based. You could draw a continuum, from connectional to congregational, and place United Methodist and other churches (Roman Catholic, Episcopal, Presbyterian, Primitive Baptist, etc.) along this continuum.

The Book of Discipline, The Book of Resolutions, and The Book of Worship

Bring copies of *The Book of Discipline, The Book of Resolutions,* and *The United Methodist Book of Worship* to this meeting. Prepare yourself to share a brief overview of each—their history, development, content, and place in our church. (Include a look at the Social Principles in The Book of Discipline as well.) Ask for questions and comments on these.

More Resources

Look at the Resources section for this chapter. The Foreword in Tom Frank's book, *Polity, Practice, and the Mission of The United Methodist Church* paints a lively picture of the relationship between United Methodist communities of faith and *The Book of Discipline.* This serves as human context for the *Discipline's* legislation and structure. If you have time, read this section (or ask one of the candidates to read it before the meeting), and share it with the group, or consider presenting a quick summary of some other book listed in this chapter's resource section.

Closing

Plan a closing time with your group. Again, you could ask for brief reactions or reflections on the group's session together. You could simply go around the group and ask for one or two words they would like to share about today's time.

Assign any homework or reading for the next meeting. Check in with individuals on their place or progress in the conference's process toward a possible certification interview with the district Committee, and to see if they have any questions about this. Use your judgment as to the best way to keep track of your group members' progress. Continue to let them know you are available to help them along the way.

Close the meeting with your group's ritual or with a time of prayer.

Part I / Chapter 3
Grace and the Sacraments

This section outlines some important theological under-standings of grace and the sacraments. Prepare for this group meeting by reading this chapter with an eye to the importance of grace for Wesley—in his life, his teachings, and in his emphasis on grace in his small groups. If you have not opted to ask candidates to do so, prepare an opening meditation or devotion for the group.

Consider opening this session by inviting group members to remember a time in their lives when they felt touched or moved by an experience of grace. Ask them to share their experience. Your own answer to this question will serve to model vulnerability as well as reinforcing the group's cov-enant to create a hospitable environment for personal and spiritual growth.

Grace

One of the major points in this chapter is the nature of grace and Wesley's understanding of three key aspects of grace: prevenient, justifying, and sanctifying. Ask for volunteers to express their understanding of one or more of these aspects. Work with the group toward identifying the role of each of these kinds of grace and integrating them into the whole experience of grace. Refer to the first three reflection questions at the end of the chapter for additional discussion entry points. A short Bible study of Psalm 59:10 (the God of mercy shall go before me) is a good way to uncover more of what it means to experience prevenient grace.

The Sacraments: Signs of Grace

Examine with the group Wesley's two signs of grace: the sacraments of baptism and Holy Communion. You may refer to the material in this chapter; you may also refer to the sections of *The Book of Discipline* that address these sacraments.

Our understanding of baptism precludes "re-baptism." Have the group reflect on why Wesley was adamant about baptism being an act of God and a sign of God's grace, not an act we do ourselves. Baptism is God's claim on us—not the other way around. Explore this carefully with candidates. Ask the group members about their baptisms—as an infant, a young person, or as an adult. One of the reflection questions asks the candidate to talk about why United Methodists baptize children. Having the ability to articulate an answer to this question will serve the candidates well as they prepare for interviews with the district Committee.

Wesley believed and taught that the communion table is open to all—believer and non-believer alike. He even taught that the sacrament of Holy Communion could in fact be a means of grace for converting non-believers: God could act on a non-believer's heart in the simple sharing of bread and wine. It is important to allow candidates to consider the difference between the practice of Wesley's "open communion" and other groups' practice of "closed communion."

"Closed communion" is the practice of restricting the serving of the elements only to those who are members in good standing of a particular denomination, church, or sect. A look at the continuum of practices could be helpful to the candidates. Consider having newsprint and markers available for candidates to make a continuum and locate different practices of Holy Communion along that continuum.

For example, the Roman Catholic Church practices closed communion, as do some confessional denominations. The Evangelical Lutheran Church in America practices "Eucharistic hospitality," which means it is the person's and not the church's decision to participate in the sacrament (though this denomination does open their table to "baptized Christians" only). Some Baptists restrict their table even more than Roman Catholics, opening it only to those who are members of their particular congregation.

Work together with your group to understand Wesley's teaching about Holy Communion. Candidates should be able to express cogently the United Methodist understanding and practice of this sacrament.

More Resources

The United Methodist Church's Board of Global Ministries website features a collection of Wesley's most important sermons. Go to the site http://www.umcmission.org/find-resources/john-wesley-sermons and find sermons in which Wesley preaches on grace, baptism, and Holy Communion. Copy excerpts to share with your group. Familiarity with some of Wesley's sermons is a good resource for candidates as they prepare for interviews. (Date accessed: June 10, 2015)

A rich variety of United Methodist theologians who have followed in Wesley's steps and embraced his thought is listed in the resources section. One book highlights the contribution of women and feminist theology. Another is the history of Hispanics/Latinos in Methodism. Two more books focus on the contributions of African-Americans and Asian-Americans in our church. If you are unable to access these and/or cannot find material on the web about these important contributions, be sure to point candidates to these books and encourage them to explore one or more.

Closing

Prepare the group to close this meeting. Ask members to share briefly one thing that stood out for them from their time with the group today. Assign any homework or reading for the next meeting. Check in with individuals on their place or progress in the conference's process toward a possible certification interview with the district Committee, and to see if they have any questions about this. Use your judgment as to the best way to keep track of your group members' progress. Continue to let them know you are available to help them along the way.

Close the meeting with your group's ritual or with a time of prayer.

Part I / Chapter 4
Spiritual Disciplines

Tending your faith—and recovering it when it gets mislaid—is fundamental to the life of a Christian. And it's especially critical for those in or considering service as ministers.

One way to open this meeting is to invite your group to talk about times when their faith has been "misplaced." What were the circumstances? How long did this period last? Who—or what—accompanied them during this time? Were there spiritual practices or disciplines that were helpful to them? How did they find their faith again—or how did their faith find them? Another way to approach this conversation is to have candidates talk in pairs or groups of three to allow additional time for sharing. Then, bring the group back together and invite candidates to share helpful spiritual practices their group discussed.

Wesley knew from personal experience how critical spiritual disciplines were as the means of grace that opened him to God's presence and leanings. He was a vocal proponent of his ministers spending time in prayer, Bible study, and giving attention to their spiritual lives. Ask the group to reflect on times in their lives when they have been especially attentive to their spiritual journey, and times when they neglected it. What differences did they notice during these times of attention or inattention? How did attention or inattention to their spirituality affect their relationships with family, friends, work, or God? How might members of this group encourage each other on the spiritual journey they share over the next few months?

Wesley and Spiritual Disciplines

Look at Wesley's division of spiritual disciplines into two categories: acts of piety and acts of mercy. As you go through his list under both kinds of acts, note Wesley's concern for both social and personal facets of spiritual formation and growth. How does this understanding match up with group members' experiences of their formation and growth? Have there been times when one facet (outward or inward) has outweighed the other?

The Rich Landscape of Spiritual Disciplines

There is richness in the variety of spiritual disciplines that feed the soul and imagination of those who seek closeness with God. This chapter explores that richness by tracing the development of different spiritual disciplines over the centuries.

As your group considers the depth and lavishness of these practices, help them keep these questions in mind:

- What does the diversity of these disciplines say about the nature of God?
- What does it say about the nature of God's relationship with these communities over the years?
- What does it say about the nature of God's relationship with individual believers?
- What does this diversity say about the spiritual lives of women and men, of different ethnic communities, and of people in different stations of life? What can group members learn about their own spiritual development from people whose lives and journeys are so diverse and so different from their own?

There are several ways you might introduce these disciplines: large or small group discussion, having one member describe what they know or have experienced with one or more of these, or leading the group in a few of the disciplines. Another way is to post summaries and instructions for each discipline around the room. Ask group members to walk around, read each one, and stand near the one that most intrigues them, feels familiar to them, or seems most unfamiliar. Then, invite group members to sit near the posted discipline they have chosen and spend 15 minutes with that discipline.

You will need to prepare for some of these stations. For *Lectio Divina*, you could provide Bibles or a passage of Scripture for people to read. Supply blank paper and pens for *Journaling*. At the *Spiritual Reading* station, provide three or four appropriate books, or have available copied excerpts from a book or two. For *Spiritual Guide*, copy excerpts from a book or article about spiritual direction.

Bring the group back together to debrief.

Closing

Prepare the group to close this meeting. Suggest that group members choose one spiritual discipline new to them to practice in the coming weeks. Ask them to journal or keep notes about the practice so they can share part of the experience with the group. Ask them to journal what part of the practice was easiest. What was most difficult? Put this exercise in the context of how critical it is to take time, constantly, to seek God and let God seek them.

Check in with individuals on their place or progress in the conference's process toward a possible certification interview with the district Committee, and to see if they have any questions about this. Use your judgment as to the best way to keep track of your group members' progress. Continue to let them know you are available to help them along the way.

Close the meeting with your group's ritual or with a time of prayer.

Part I / Chapter 5
Vocation, Call, and Gifts

"Our vocation is not a sphinx's riddle, which we must solve in one guess or else perish." Thomas Merton, a Trappist monk writing about vocation, asserts that finding our vocation is not a game of hide-and-seek with God, but a two-way interaction between God and us. Open this session with Merton's quote and encourage the group to talk about its implications for them.

Vocation and Call

This chapter speaks to the heart of what it means to be called to a vocation. Here are the major elements of call in this chapter:

- the call from Scripture (with a focus on Zacchaeus, Samuel, and Mary)
- Wesley's understanding of call (through the *Historic Three Questions* and the role of these questions in the district Committee interview)
- Jesus's struggle with call (and his relationship with God through the Holy Spirit)

Be prepared to lead your group in discussion and interaction around these issues. Help them make personal connections with these elements of call.

Gifts

Look over the questions in this section. Use these questions, or others you think are helpful, either in a whole group discussion or in smaller groups or pairs. What came up during the discussion? Highlight reflections on accomplishments, possessions, values, energy, or boredom for work. How do these inform candidates as they seek to discern their calls?

Where Gifts Begin

This section addresses the complex nature of who we are and what we might bring to ministry because of it. Family of origin, family of choice, current family and primary relationships, community of support, sex and gender, race, ethnicity, our bodies, and our socioeconomic background interact in myriad ways to shape who we are. Ask candidates to talk about these questions: Which of the factors have most influenced the development of their gifts? Which had the most positive effect on their gifts? Which get in the way of letting them claim their gifts? What effects do body, health, gender, race, and economic or social status have?

Helping candidates identify the factors that shape their gifts will be important. Figuring out how they are put together and how both their past and present circumstances and relationships contribute to their identity is a crucial step in the process of discernment. This kind of self-understanding will enable them to grow, as well as avoid potential pitfalls that might lie ahead. Use your best judgment about how to structure the candidates' interactions with these nine questions; the time you devote to this will matter a great deal.

Triumph and Shortfall: Valuing Others' Perspectives

The saying is true: if you want someone to get to know you, share three triumphs with them; if you want someone to get to know you better, share three shortfalls. This is the place where community feedback, affirmation, and critique come into play for candidates. This section includes approaches for helping the group critique and support each other. Emphasize the importance of looking honestly at their abilities, their performance, and the strengths and weaknesses of their gifts.

Honest self-examination is an integral part of preparing candidates for ministry. Share this, and your support, with your candidacy group.

Closing

Prepare the group to close the meeting. Assign any homework or reading for the next meeting. Check in with individuals on their place or progress in the conference's process toward a possible certification interview with the district Committee, and to see if they have any questions about this. Use your judgment as to the best way to keep track of your group members' progress. Continue to let them know you are available to help them along the way.

Close the meeting with your group's ritual or with a time of prayer.

Part I / Chapter 6
Same Spirit, Many Callings

"Many people labor under the impression that those who work for the church—missionaries, consecrated lay ministers, licensed or ordained clergy—have a higher calling than those who work in other professions and jobs." This quote from the chapter is a widely held belief and one most candidates would have heard, and may even believe. Using the Scriptures and church history cited below, lead your group through a discussion that will help them place "church" work alongside other kinds of work as God-given and holy. You might do this by:

- Looking at the juxtaposition in Luke of the stories of Mary and Martha alongside the Good Samaritan. What do these stories say about the nature of callings?
- Relate biblical calls to church-related work. Aaron and his sons were called to the priesthood; Mary was called to bear Christ into the world; Simon and Andrew were called from fishing to supporting Jesus's work and evangelizing; and Barnabas, Saul, and John were called to proclaim the word of God in synagogues.
- Examine the many examples in the Bible of God calling people to non-church-related work. Joshua was called to be a military and political leader; David was called to become king during a crisis in Israel; Esther was called as queen to risk her life to save her people; and businesswoman Lydia was called to provide financial support to the new Christian community.

End this portion of the session by focusing on these words from the chapter: "Keep in your mind and heart that, whatever your profession—whether it was something you did or did not have a choice in—the calling is to full-time service." What effect does this have on candidates as they discern their callings? What effect do these statements have on candidates' attitudes toward "church-related" and "non-church-related" work?

Deacons, Elders, and Local Pastors

Ask the group to focus on the differences—sacramental, functional, day-to-day—among deacons, elders, and local pastors. What are these? In what ways are these three most similar? In what ways are they most different? What most distinguishes each from the other two?

Find out which of the short vignettes of deacons, elders, and local pastors each candidate most identified with or found most intriguing. What was it that struck them about one or two of the stories? Which looked most challenging to them? Which felt more familiar or comfortable?

Taking Time to Reflect

After these discussions, lead your group in a time of personal reflection. Gather them in silence and invite them to center for quiet prayer and contemplation on today's discussion. Guide them through an extended meditation. You may want to use some of the following as prompts:

Consider your own gifts and present circumstances.

- What feelings and thoughts come when you consider being at work in the world
  > as a lay person,
  > as a deacon,
  > as an elder,
  > or as a local pastor?
- Imagine yourself on each of these paths. What might your work look like as a deacon? An elder? A local pastor? As a faithful Christian in a setting outside traditional ordained or licensed ministry?
- What appeals to you about each of these? What gives you pause? Why? What is least enticing?

- To which form of ministry are you most attracted? Why? Which feels as though it might fit you well?
- Think about God and God's presence in your life. Sit quietly and listen for anything God might be telling you right now.

Give candidates time to ponder these questions. Then, call them back together. If there are those who wish to share something of their prayer experience, invite them to do so. But remind them that this reflection was simply a time for them and God and that keeping the time private is fine.

Closing

Prepare the group to close the meeting. Assign any homework or reading for the next meeting. Check in with individuals on their place or progress in the conference's process toward a possible certification interview with the district Committee, and to see if they have any questions about this. Use your judgment as to the best way to keep track of your group members' progress. Continue to let them know you are available to help them along the way.

Close the meeting with your group's ritual or with a time of prayer.

Part I / Chapter 7
Yes, No, Maybe: Health and Wholeness

If you are not familiar with Wesley's *Primitive Physick: Or An Easy and Natural Way of Curing Most Diseases*, you might peruse it in preparation for this session. The preface is reproduced on the website of the General Board of Global Ministries of The

United Methodist Church, as listed in the chapter's resource section. Choose a few passages from it to open this session. Wesley was very interested in health and wholeness; some of his observations are useful and stand the test of time. Others are simply entertaining.

This section addresses health and wholeness—physical, emotional, and behavioral. Helping candidates address their own health and encouraging them to consider ways to become or stay healthy are the major issues here. Begin by discussing with your group our Christian and Wesleyan roots in holistic care and how entering licensed or ordained ministry might affect their personal care practices.

Physical Health and Abilities

Being or becoming physically healthy requires thought, time, and effort. Caring for the body is a spiritual discipline. This means being connected and aware, living through the body, and not just living in it. (The concept of soma informs the conversation here.)

Healthy eating, regular exercise, and adequate rest strengthen our health and can improve our quality of life. Address these with your group. How well are they addressing these physical issues? How often are they connected with their bodies? How well do they listen to what their bodies need?

"*The Book of Discipline* is clear: a disability is not considered an unfavorable health factor (¶324.8). What matters is your ability to meet the professional standards and to render effective service in your appointment setting." Go over this statement from the chapter, highlighting its meaning for those who are differently abled and for our perspectives on ability and disability. Clarify the church's position that what matters most about a candidate's health is their ability to be effective in service as a minister.

Emotional Health

Coping with stress, fostering the ability to understand and manage feelings, and practicing adaptability in the midst of change are some of the challenges candidates face in everyday life—and some of the challenges they will face in their lives as ministers.

Give your group time to examine various aspects of caring for their emotional health. Encourage them to discuss which practices are relatively familiar to them and which present particular challenges. Ask people to share their own habits or suggestions for becoming more emotionally healthy in these areas. Help them understand that the district Committee will address these issues with them in their interviews.

Behavioral Health

Become familiar, if you are not already, with the *Behavioral Health Guidelines* by the General Board of Higher Education and Ministry of The United Methodist Church. These were written to help conference Boards of Ordained Ministry address behavioral health as it relates to effectiveness in ministry and the avoidance of misconduct. This resource assists boards in the selection of candidates for ministry. These guidelines are available on the Board of Ordained Ministry Library at www.bomlibrary.org.

Behavioral health as part of holistic health is critical, yet it is one of the more difficult health measures to talk about and address. Talk with your group about the behavioral health categories. How would good health in each of those categories affect ministry? How would disruption in each of those categories affect ministry in a congregation?

Spiritual Health

For many, taking a full Sabbath is a major point of resistance. Slowing down is difficult. Over-commitment is an easy rhythm to fall into. Learning how to rest in a world that encourages us to go faster and faster, to produce and consume more and more as a sign of success, is no easy task. Ask your group if any of them practice Sabbath. What does this look like—is it a full day each week, or an hour each day? What do they do to maintain boundaries when life gets busy? Are there any candidates who do not practice Sabbath, or feel they cannot? Ask them what impedes them? How might they find rest each day, rather than taking a full day each week?

A Life of Health and Balance

The context for getting healthy and staying healthy is not just the individual. Consider this statement from the chapter: ". . . the responsibility for your health is not yours alone. The local church (or other setting) in which you serve has a responsibility, too. They are, in fact, partners in this endeavor with you. They can help in a variety of ways." What are the implications of this statement? How does your group react to this? Are they surprised? Skeptical? Encouraged?

Talk with your group about the importance of understanding their needs in the many areas of health, as well as finding ways to articulate that to others. Can they see themselves being able to do that, or would they have trouble asking for what they need? Explore with candidates what it means to ask others—family, church, friends—for what they need.

Closing

Prepare the group to close this meeting. Suggest that each group member choose one specific area of health to be mindful of in the coming week. Also, tell candidates to look ahead to the next chapter, and point them to the "Planning for Ministry Financial Worksheet" on page 124. Ask them to complete this worksheet in preparation for your next meeting.

Check in with individuals on their place or progress in the conference's process toward a possible certification interview with the district Committee, and to see if they have any questions about this. Use your judgment as to the best way to keep track of your group members' progress. Continue to let them know you are available to help them along the way.

Close the meeting with your group's ritual or with a time of prayer.

Part I / Chapter 8
Yes, No, Maybe: Financial Literacy

Discussing money can be sensitive, complicated, and even problematic. But for candidates, financial literacy is essential.

Start with a non-threatening exercise. Divide the group into threes. Ask them to discuss these questions:

- Are you comfortable talking about your financial situation?
- What attitudes and approaches to money did you learn from your family of origin?
- If you are married or in a relationship, who handles the finances? How did you decide on that approach? How is it working? If you are single, are you the only person

in charge of your finances? How long have you been financially independent?

- Are you more of a spender or a saver? What did you see modeled as you were growing up in the area of finances?
- How does your faith influence your decisions about money?
- What discoveries or insights have you gained as you have thought about your finances?
- Have you ever made and used a budget?
- What part does charitable giving play in your life?

After the small groups have had time to discuss these, bring everyone back together. Find out what the experience was like for them and ask them to share something from their group.

Goals: Today and Tomorrow

The ability to articulate personal and professional goals will help candidates gain clarity as circumstances change and will serve them well during the discernment process, as well as in the future. Give your group a chance to reflect on their goals.

Encourage them to consider these four requisites to setting and achieving goals:

- Identify the financial costs of achieving these goals.
- Make a timeline that includes steps along the way to the goals.
- Ask for help—scholarships, loans, ways to reduce spending.
- Remember the big picture; be honest and open; talk with others about goals as they evolve and change.

Theology and Psychology of Money

In this section there are several key areas. First, the origins of candidates' attitudes and approaches to money most likely surfaced in the previous group conversation. In addition, theological convictions about debt, spending, and giving are key to understanding money. Share how these factors are critical to financial literacy. Since this particular discussion may make some candidates feel uneasy, remind the group that no one is required to share anything they do not want to.

A Closer Look

Developing a healthy financial plan requires becoming aware of and paying attention to a variety of economic elements: spending, income, borrowing, additional funding. Find out where members of your group stood in their awareness of these elements of their finances before they filled out the worksheet and where they stand now that they have completed it. What changed? How do they see their own financial situation right now, as they consider seminary, graduate school, or Course of Study (or continue in those studies, if already started)? What areas of concern do they have in providing for themselves, family members, or other dependents in the next few years? What resources can they identify for additional funding? (If you are aware of other resources, share those.)

Closing

Prepare the group to close the meeting. Check in with individuals on their place or progress in the conference's process toward a possible certification interview with the district Committee, and to see if they have any questions about this.

Use your judgment as to the best way to keep track of your group members' progress. Continue to let them know you are available to help them along the way.

Close the meeting with your group's ritual or with a time of prayer.

Part I / Chapter 9
Yes, No, Maybe: Next Steps

It is time for candidates to make decisions. Will they apply for certification as a candidate? Will they decide instead to continue their ministry as a layperson? Are they undecided, unsure of where they are being called to go next?

As a mentor, your role has been significant in this process. It is even more so now. How will you facilitate these candidates—whose journeys are so varied and whose decisions will be so varied—as they listen even more closely for God's direction and will? Praying—for them and yourself—is vital.

But you, like the candidates, are not alone. God has promised you the Spirit's presence, even as you have promised to be present to the candidates. Rely on the Spirit and place yourself in God's care as you care for these candidates.

Consider how you will structure this session. The decisions candidates make now require both one-on-one time with you as well as time with the group. The size of your group, the parameters of time, and your own availability will factor into how you address this next step.

If you meet one-on-one with each candidate before the group meets, discuss with them where they are in their decision-making. You may want to schedule these individual times after the group has met for the last time in order to follow up with each candidate about their decision. Or you may want to lead the group halfway through the session, break to spend one-on-one time with candidates, then call the group back together to discuss candidates' decisions. If logistics preclude doing any of these, consider dividing the group meeting into two separate sessions and meet individual candidates in the time between the two sessions. Whatever you (and the group, to the extent you are able to involve them) decide, make sure the major points below are part of the plan.

Gaining Clarity

Begin your group meeting with the questions in this section. These questions address group members' images of their call, the feedback that has helped them better understand their call, the place of their ego in hearing God's intention for them, and any conversations they may need to have to get a clearer answer to their call.

Consider breaking into small groups to discuss these questions, and then return to the large group for debriefing. Or allow time for candidates to engage these questions by journaling privately, and then ask them to share their observations and insights with the whole group.

Remind the group that everyone's call or decision is unique, and though that call may look different from anyone else's, it is still a valid call. Encourage candidates to value and trust their own relationship with God—again, God's relationship with each of us is uncommonly singular.

Three Possibilities Ahead

Lead your group in the exercise in this section. If they have not yet done so, ask candidates to summarize their call in one or two sentences on an index card. As each person reads their summary aloud, ask the group to give them feedback. How do group members see that person's gifts for ministry in the context of what that candidate has written about their own call? How do reactions from the group reinforce or challenge what the candidate has said about their call? Follow the group's discussion to help them give effective and comprehensive feedback to each other.

Honoring Passages

Marking the beginning or end of a season with a ritual can be a profound way to honor candidates' decisions and choices. Together with your group, come up with a short ritual or liturgy to send them forth. Find a way to bless, as a worshipping community, the next steps each will undertake in the coming weeks and months. Honor the covenant you made with your group at the beginning of this process with a final pledge of continued support.

Next Steps

Find ways to accompany members of your group in their next steps. If their answer was "no," discuss with them what their next steps will be in discerning their call. If their answer is "maybe," discuss what next steps might be. If their answer is "yes," work with them to begin the next steps they will take in order to meet with the district Committee regarding certified candidacy. Whatever their decision, be careful to work out a follow-up plan that makes sense for each group member and the particular requirements in your conference.

Mentor's Report

As a mentor, you have responsibilities both to the candidates in your group and to the wider Church. You covenanted to serve the group in its discernment process; you also covenanted to serve the Church by helping candidates discern how they can best serve.

Now it is time to write a mentor report for each of your group members. These written reports are shared with the district Committee on Ordained Ministry. Keep in mind this report is introductory and informational. It highlights the candidate's understanding of their own gifts, grace, and calling for ministry, as well as issues the candidate may need to explore further. This report is not evaluative or supervisory; it is relevant to the candidate's experience thus far in their preparation for ministry.

As a mentor, you prepare this report and share it with the candidate before sending it to the district Committee on Ordained Ministry. You and the candidate together will consent to the contents of the report and will each sign the report before sending it to the district Committee. It will not contain any confidential information without the candidate's permission. In fact, no conversation or personal information will be shared unless the candidate gives written permission. Mutual respect and confidentiality are the baseline for the report.

Share with your group some of the facets of this one-page report: the candidate's self-awareness, gifts for ministry, articulation of call, and your observation of their faith journey thus far. Answer any questions they may have about the mentor's report.

Consider the following questions as you prepare the mentor report:

- What is this person's self-understanding in relation to a possible call and career in ministry?
- What gifts does this person have for licensed or ordained ministry, and how have you observed evidence of grace in their life, and what is this person's understanding of how she or he hopes to serve in licensed or ordained ministry in The United Methodist Church?
- How do they understand their call from God into licensed or ordained ministry? Can they clearly articulate an understanding of that call?
- How have they responded to the information and content about the call and work of an ordained or licensed minister in The United Methodist Church?
- How has their understanding of their call been affirmed by others?
- Have they honored their covenant with the group to be present, open, and involved in the group's process?
- How do they respond to feedback from others? Have they given others helpful feedback?
- How do they understand their spiritual life? What spiritual disciplines have they experienced during these last weeks? What disciplines seem to undergird them in their daily lives?
- What other comments, factors, or suggestions can you, as their mentor, offer that might be important for the district Committee's consideration?

Also, be sure to check with your conference's candidacy registrar to see if there is a conference standard form for you to prepare for candidates.

Your Time and Commitment

The time, energy, and commitment you have invested in the lives of those exploring ministry have the potential to affect the spiritual lives of these candidates for a lifetime. Your efforts also shape the future of your annual conference and of United Methodism. You may see some of the fruits of your work and be gratified and humbled. In other instances, you will probably never know the extent of your influence. But all your efforts—and the efforts of all the candidates—are seen as blessed by God.

Appendix B
Candicacy Process Checklists

Note: While all of these steps must be completed, you will need to check with your mentor and annual conference with questions about sequence and the process for various steps. Your annual conference may also have additional requirements that are not listed here. Confirm all requirements for candidacy, licensing, and ordination with your annual conference.

To Become a Certified Candidate (¶ 310)
Complete ✔

1. Obtain a high school diploma or its equivalency _____

2. Be a member of The United Methodist Church, or an active, baptized participant in a United Methodist ministry setting, for at least one year. _____

3. Read *The Christian as Minister*, then talk with your pastor, collegiate minister, or another deacon, elder, or local pastor about your call. _____

4. Receive charge conference approval (church or other approved ministry setting) to enter the candidacy process. _____

5. Write to district superintendent outlining call and desire to enter Candidacy (may also include meeting with district Committee). _____

6. District superintendent (or other appointed officer) enters candidate into UMCARES*, selects "Candidacy Track" & "Psychological Assessment Track" (as appropriate). _____

7. District superintendent (or other appointed officer) assigns mentor via UMCARES. _____

8. Applicant receives email invitation from UMCARES to register. _____

9. Mentor receives email notification from UMCARES assigning candidate. _____

10. District superintendent approves candidate's application via UMCARES. _____

11. Candidate pays application fee and receives Candidacy Guidebook. _____

12. Meet with mentor (individually or with group). _____

13. Complete criminal background check, credit check, and psychological assessment. _____

14. Mentor submits report to district Committee before candidate interviews for certification. _____

15. Agree to live according to the highest ideals of the Christian life, as set forth in ¶¶ 101–104 and ¶¶ 160–166 (Social Principles). _____

16. Request to interview for certified candidacy with the district Committee and receive 3/4 approval of district Committee to become certified (written ballot, ¶ 666.6). _____

17. Mentor, candidacy registrar, or Board of Ordained Ministry staff indicates certification approval/denial in UMCARES. _____

18. Receive annual charge conference and district Committee approval to continue as a certified candidate. _____

To Become a Local Pastor and Be Licensed (¶ 315)
Complete ✔

1. Become a certified candidate.   _____

2. Complete the Board of Ordained Ministry-
   sponsored "Orientation to Ministry" (¶ 312).   _____

3. Successfully complete Licensing School or
   1/3 of a Master of Divinity degree.   _____

4. Be recommended by the district Committee
   for initial license and annual approval; receive
   appointment from the Bishop.   _____

To Become an Associate Member (¶ 322)
Complete ✔

1. Minimum 40 years of age with four years of
   service as a full-time local pastor (or equivalent). _____

2. Complete the Course of Study and a minimum
   of 60 hours toward a bachelor's degree
   (or equivalent).   _____

3. Be recommended by the district Committee
   and the Board of Ordained Ministry.   _____

4. Accept a full-time continuing appointment. _____

5. Satisfy the Board of Ordained Ministry physical health requirements, psychological reports, and criminal background and credit checks. _____

6. Complete a written doctrinal exam (¶ 324.9) and prepare a written sermon on suggested Bible passage. _____

7. Receive clergy session approval. _____

To Become a Provisional Member via Course of Study (¶ 324.6)
Complete ✔

1. Be a minimum of 40 years of age. _____

2. Satisfy all requirements of Sections 1–3 and 7–14 of ¶ 324. _____

3. Complete bachelor's degree. _____

4. Complete the Course of Study, with no more than 1/2 taken online or via correspondence. _____

5. Complete Advanced Course of Study through a University Senate-approved seminary. _____

6. Submit an autobiographical statement and written doctrinal exam to the Board of Ordained Ministry.   _____

7. Present certificate of good health and Candidate's Disclosure Form 114.   _____

8. Be interviewed by the district Committee and recommended in writing to the Board of Ordained Ministry by a 3/4 majority vote of the district Committee.   _____

9. Be interviewed by the Board of Ordained Ministry and recommended to the clergy session by a 2/3 majority vote of the Board of Ordained Ministry (¶ 324.14).   _____

10. Receive clergy session approval.   _____

To Become a Provisional Member via Master's Degree (¶ 324)
Complete ✔

1. Be a certified candidate for at least one year, maximum 12 years (¶ 324.1).   _____

2. Demonstrate gifts for ministry of service and leadership to the district Committee's satisfaction (¶ 324.2).   _____

3. Be interviewed by the district Committee
    and recommended in writing to the Board of
    Ordained Ministry by a 3/4 majority vote
    of the district Committee (¶ 324.10).   _____

4. Complete BOM-sponsored "Orientation
    to Ministry" (¶ 312).   _____

5. Complete bachelor's degree.   _____

6. Complete 1/2 of the Master of Divinity degree
    (deacon or elder), or 1/2 of a master's degree
    in a specialized field plus 1/2 of the Basic
    Graduate Theological Studies (deacon).   _____

7. Present certificate of good health and
    Candidate's Disclosure Form 114.   _____

8. Submit an autobiographical statement and a
    written doctrinal exam to the Board of
    Ordained Ministry.   _____

9. Be interviewed by the Board of Ordained
    Ministry and recommended to the clergy
    session by 2/3 majority vote of the Board
    (¶ 324.14).   _____

10. Receive clergy session approval.   _____

To Become a Full Member: Deacon (¶ 330) or Elder (¶ 335)

Complete ✔

1. Serve under appointment for at least two full annual conference years. _____

2. Been previously elected as a provisional member. _____

3. Complete educational requirements: Master of Divinity (deacon or elder); or a master's degree in a specialized field, plus the Basic Graduate Theological Studies (deacon). _____

4. Respond to a written or oral doctrinal exam administered by the Board of Ordained Ministry. _____

5. Present a project demonstrating fruitfulness carrying out church's mission of "Making Disciples of Jesus Christ for the Transformation of the World." _____

6. Apply to and interview with the Board of Ordained Ministry to receive a 2/3 majority approval of Board's recommendation for ordination. _____

7. Receive 2/3 majority approval of clergy session, participate in ordination service, and be ordained by a bishop. _____

UMCARES is the United Methodist Candidate and Record Entry System. Once your district superintendent (or another appointed annual conference officer) invites you to register in the system, this is where you will note your completion of various tasks and steps in the candidacy process.

Appendix C
Candicacy Retreat Examples

Example 1

Pre-Retreat (evening before retreat begins)
6:00 PM	Mentor Dinner
7:00 PM	Retreat Briefing

Retreat Day One
9:00 AM	Participant Check-In & Photograph
9:30 AM	Fellowship with Small Groups
10:00 AM	Opening Worship
11:15 AM	Orientation to Ministry
12:30 PM	Lunch with Small Groups
1:30 PM	Workshops
2:30 PM	Break/Refreshments
2:45 PM	Workshops
3:45 PM	Coffee with District Leadership
4:45 PM	Break / Lodging Check-In

| 6:00 PM | Dinner |
| 7:00 PM | Candidacy Group Session |

Retreat Day Two

8:00 AM	Breakfast
8:30 AM	Worship
10:00 AM	Candidacy Group Session
12:15 PM	Lunch
1:00 PM	Psychological Assessment
4:00 - 6:00 PM	Departure

Example 2

Retreat Day One

1:00 PM	Opening Worship
3:00 PM	Large Group Info Session
4:00 PM	Workshops
6:00 PM	Dinner
7:00 PM	Candidacy Groups
8:30 PM	Lodging Check-In

Retreat Day Two

8:00 AM	Breakfast
8:30 AM	Gathering and Prayer
9:30 AM	Psychological Assessments
12:30 PM	Lunch with Candidacy Groups
2:00 PM	Prayer and Sending Forth

Example 3

Retreat Day One

3:00 PM	Participant Check-In and Photograph
4:30 PM	Opening Worship
6:00 PM	Dinner with Your District
7:00 PM	Exploring Mentor Groups
9:00 PM	Lodging Check-In

Retreat Day Two

8:00 AM	Breakfast
9:00 AM	Worship
9:30 AM	Candidacy Overview (Skit)
10:30 AM	Workshops A
11:15 AM	Workshops B
12:00 PM	Lunch with Your District
1:00 PM	Setup and Training for Psychological Assessment
2:00 PM	Psychological Assessments
6:00 PM	Dinner
7:00 PM	Mentor Groups— Candidacy Guidebook

Retreat Day Three

8:00 AM	Breakfast and Check-Out
9:00 AM	Mentor Groups— Behavioral Health Guidelines and Next Steps
11:00 AM	Worship
12:00 PM	Lunch
1:00 PM	Conclude

Endnotes

[1] Fr. William Saunders, "The Symbolism of the Pelican," *Catholic Education Resource Center*, accessed January 12, 2016, http://www.catholiceducation.org/en/culture/catholic-contributions/the-symbolism-of-the-pelican.html.

[2] John Schuster, *Answering Your Call: A Guide to Living Your Deepest Purpose* (San Francisco, CA: Berrett-Koehler, 2003), 47.

[3] John Neafsey, *A Sacred Voice is Calling: Personal Vocation and Social Conscience* (Maryknoll, NY: Orbis Books, 2006), 25.

[4] All biblical references use the Common English Bible translation unless otherwise noted.

[5] *The Book of Discipline of The United Methodist Church, 2012* (Nashville, TN: United Methodist Publishing House, 2012). All references to *The Book of Discipline* refer to the 2012 edition unless otherwise noted.

[6] Willie James Jennings, "The Fuller Difference: To Be a Christian Intellectual," accessed November 17, 2015, https://fullermag.fuller.edu/the-fuller-difference-to-be-a-christian-intellectual.

[7] "The Letters of John Wesley," *The Wesley Center Online*, accessed November 17, 2015, http://wesley.nnu.edu/john-wesley/the-letters-of-john-wesley/wesleys-letters-1768.

[8] From this point forward, all paragraph citations from *The Book of Discipline* will be cited parenthetically using ¶.

[9] *The Book of Resolutions of The United Methodist Church, 2012* (Nashville, TN: United Methodist Publishing House, 2012). All references to The Book of Resolutions refer to the 2012 edition unless otherwise noted.

[10] Gerald G. May, *The Awakened Heart: Opening Yourself to the Love You Need* (New York: HarperCollins, 1991), 54.

[11] Mary Karr, "Disgraceland," in *Sinners Welcome: Poems* (New York: Harper Perennial, 2009), 6. Accessed November 17, 2015, http://www.poetryfoundation.org/poetrymagazine/poem/31279.

[12] Discipleship Ministries. "Teaching grace in Christian education," *UMC.org*, accessed November 17, 2015, http://www.umc.org/resources/teaching-grace-in-christian-education.

[13] R. Maurice Boyd, *A Lover's Quarrel with the World*, ed. Ian A. Hunter (Burlington, Ontario: Welch Publishing Company, Inc., 1985), 74.

[14] Ralph C. Wood, *The Comedy of Redemption: Christian Faith and Comic Vision in Four American Novelists* (Notre Dame, IN: University of Notre Dame Press, 1988), 230.

15 Wood, 230–231.

16 *The United Methodist Hymnal*, (Nashville, TN: The United Methodist Publishing House, 1989), 7.

17 Louise Penny, *Bury Your Dead: A Chief Inspector Gamache Novel* (New York: Minotaur Books, 2011), 170.

18 Carol Ann Duffy, "Prayer," in *Mean Time* (London: Anvil Press, 1993), 52.

19 Thomas Merton, *No Man Is an Island* (New York: Mariner Books, 2002), 131.

20 Ellen Johnson Sirleaf. "Text of Ellen Johnson Sirleaf's Speech," *Harvard Gazette*, Last modified May 26, 2011, date accessed November 19, 2015, http://news.harvard.edu/gazette/story/2011/05/text-of-ellen-johnson-sirleaf%E2%80%99s-speech/.

21 Marge Piercy, "To be of use," in *Circles on the Water: Selected Poems of Marge Piercy* (New York: Alfred A. Knopf, Inc., 1982), 106.

22 Frederick Buechner, *Wishful Thinking: A Theological ABC* (New York: Harper and Row, 1973), 95.

23 Khalil Gibran, *The Prophet* (New York: Alfred A. Knoph, 1923), 36.

24 "Mary and Martha" (Luke 10:38–42), *Theology of Work*, accessed October 10, 2014, http://www.theologyofwork.org/.

25 Margaret Ann Crain, *The United Methodist Deacon: Ordained to Word, Service, Compassion, and Justice* (Nashville, TN: Abingdon Press, 2014), 121.

26 Crain, 102.

27 As quoted in Kathleen McAlpin, *Ministry That Transforms: A Contemplative Process of Theological Reflection* (Collegeville, MN: Liturgical Press, 2009), 10.

28 Kate Braestrup, *Here If You Need Me: A True Story*, (New York: Little, Brown and Company, 2007), 60.

29 Wesley to Alexander Knox, 26 October 1778, in *The Letters of the Rev. John Wesley, A.M.*, ed. John Telford (London: Epworth, 1931), 6:327.

30 Barbara Brown Taylor, *An Altar in the World: A Geography of Faith* (New York: HarperOne, 2009), 130.

31 Taylor, 121.

32 Taylor, 139.

33 Peter Lynch, *Beating the Street* (New York: Simon and Schuster, 1994), 305.

34 "Loan Calculator," *FinAid*, accessed, September 11, 2014, http://www.finaid.org/calculators/loanpayments.phtml.

35 "Deferment and Forbearance," *Federal Student Aid*, accessed September 11, 2014, https://studentaid.ed.gov/repay-loans/deferment-forbearance.

36 John Wesley, "The Use of Money," *Global Ministries: The United Methodist Church*, accessed May 28, 2015, http://www.umcmission.org/Find-Resources/John-Wesley-Sermons/Sermon-50-The-Use-of-Money.

37 Annie Dillard, "Living like Weasels," in *Touchstone Anthology of Contemporary Creative Nonfiction: Work from 1970 to Present*, ed. Lex Williford and Michael Martone (New York: Simon & Schuster, 2007), 151.

38 Howard Thurman, *A Strange Freedom: The Best of Howard Thurman on Religious Experience and Public Life*, ed. Walter Earl Fluker and Catherine Tumber (Boston: Beacon Press, 1998), 31.

CPSIA information can be obtained
at www.ICGtesting.com
Printed in the USA
FFOW02n0211130117
31282FF